I Want Somebody to Know My Name

D0921073

I Want Somebody to Know My Name

Catherine Meeks

Smyth & Helwys Publishing, Inc.®
Macon, Georgia

ISBN 1-880837-78-1

I Want Somebody to Know My Name
Cathy Meeks

Copyright © 1994
Smyth & Helwys Publishing, Inc.®
Macon, Georgia

All rights reserved.

Printed in the United States of America.

The paper used in this publication meets the minimum
requirements of American Standard for Information
Sciences—Permanence of paper for Printed Library Material,
ANSI Z39.48-1984

Library of Congress Cataloging-in-Publication Data

Meeks, Cathy
    I want somebody to know my name/Cathy Meeks–Rev. ed.
      xiv + 114   6" x 9" (15 x 23 cm.)
      Includes index.
      ISBN 1-880837-78-1   (alk. paper)
      1. Meeks, Cathy, 2. Christian biography–United States,
      3. Afro-Americans–Biography. I. Title.
      BR1725.M358A34 1994   209'.2–dc20
                                            [B]
                                  94-13426
                                          CIP

Contents

Foreword

In the midst of my own busy writing life, I am asked often (sometimes too often!) to write a foreword for another author's book. In this instance, though, I jumped at the chance to find out if I was capable of writing one for a book as unusual and provocative as *I Want Somebody to Know My Name*. Let me say at the outset that Catherine Meeks is not only a lucid, colorful writer, but an authentic thinker—an authentic Christian thinker, who looks at life in a way that keeps reminding me of the very nature of Jesus Christ himself. As with us all, Cathy Meeks is not a perfect human being, but with His promptings, she does her level best to *love*. She also *thinks*, and when her own thinking indicates that she is not quite expressing the mind of Christ, she is humanly intelligent enough to see the difference—to see where her own keen human mind has taken over. She also has the courage to allow Him to change her thinking until it more closely resembles "the mind of Christ."

Although we have known each other for some fifteen years, too much "busyness" has kept us from sharing thoughts and beliefs for some time, and, yet—when she called the other day—I felt as though we had been together almost constantly. The truth is, I felt even more comfortable with her than I had all those years ago. Count back to a time before a change of administrations in Washington brought on an almost abrupt lack of general interest in racial issues, before a rash of assassinations—almost before we realized it—divided our country. I hope that we will come together again now, but we are still divided. So I am doubly grateful that Smyth and Helwys Publishing Company is once more making this important book available to everyone. African-American or white —we all need it, perhaps more than we needed it fifteen years ago.

A careful, thoughtful reading of *I Want Somebody to Know My Name* can change us all and bring us all home again to the place of freedom within ourselves—black and white—where we can truly rest and work and play and think together in God's nature.

The most significant gift of the life in Christ is *forgiveness*. No other great religion offers forgiveness because none reveals the very heart and intention of God as Jesus does. The following is one potent paragraph from Meeks' book that struck me so forcefully while reading the pages again fifteen years later. (I felt as though I had missed it entirely the first time.)

> We need to start by accepting our forgiveness. We need desperately to get beyond that slave/slavemaster mentality we have all inherited. White people have to forgive themselves and their ancestors for their heritage, and blacks need to do the same (i.e., forgive whites alive today who had no active part in the dreadful system). We *are* forgiven, and it is time we started acting like it.

I have just finished reading these pages for the third time. I will read them again and again, and I fully expect to continue learning. For example, in some groups it is "politically correct" now for the races to live separately—for whites to know their culture, for blacks to concentrate only on theirs. Cathy wrote all those years ago that blacks need to ask "Who am I?" instead of "Who are *we*?" I smiled during this reading of the book when I realized that she had said how sick she is of blacks and whites contending that they have nothing in common, when no stronger bond can ever be found than Christ himself!

There are gems like these on almost every page, plus the riveting (though all too common) story of a young black girl who opened herself to allow God to free her—all the way. People know the name of Catherine Meeks now, not only because she lectures widely and teaches at one of our great universities but because her inner-liberation shows. As she also wrote, those of us who dare to try it find the lordship of Christ much like slavery, except that if we are really under the lordship of Christ, we are all free.

I need freedom as much as any black person on earth needs it. I even need it especially in my chosen career as a historical novelist working in the nineteenth century when almost every black person in the United States was a slave. I need Christ's freeing in order to lose my timidity to write my black characters as whole people. Christ is giving it to me. As long as I live on this earth, I expect to receive more and more liberty, not only to be myself but to allow those I know—of whatever race—to be themselves.

My friend, Cathy Meeks, will go on helping me understand how to receive the freedom of God because she will go right on learning to understand it herself. You will miss too much if you miss reading *I Want Somebody to Know My Name.*

Eugenia Price
St. Simons Island, Georgia

Foreword

In our American society, culture plays perhaps one of the most influential roles in our lives. For the black person, this can be an immensely frustrating realization. Since we are far removed from our original African culture, we are faced with a struggle to either delude ourselves by accepting an identity parallel to an Anglo-Saxon social-image, or to reach out, find, and identify ourselves with what we believe to be real and truly meaningful to us as human beings.

As a child, Cathy Meeks's life was a carbon copy of many black youngsters' who have grown up in the shadow of parents who believed that life for blacks in America had to be a hopeless entity and that the best way to live through it was to be passive and nonresistant to the harnesses imposed on them by the dominant society. Her father failed to instill in her any values that meant "you are a person" or "you are just as important and capable as anyone else." Subsequently, when she went to college and a white instructor placed demands on her to achieve, Cathy immediately felt that he was being cold-hearted and racist, for she had been deluded into believing that she was inferior and could not achieve on a level equivalent to whites.

I Want Somebody to Know My Name probes beyond the depths of theological teachings and proves that having a right relationship with God can help people to establish new images of themselves. Through the soul-healing power of God, Cathy realized that she was not inferior to anyone, that she could achieve, and that she could make a mark upon her world.

I recommend that you read *I Want Somebody to Know My Name.* This testimony shows how the reconciling power of God can ascend color barriers and help to make the body whole.

John Perkins
Voice of Calvary Ministries
Jackson, Mississippi

Preface

When I was a college student, I often wished for black persons who had both love for God and a commitment to social action. I wanted to know black persons who had the courage to allow Jesus to be Lord in spite of our heritage of slavery. I found no one to meet my needs.

As a result of this lack of black models, I decided to try to become that person myself. I wanted to become a person not only deeply committed to God, but also a person involved in social action—a social action motivated by love for God and not by the possibility of personal gain. I have written this book in an attempt partially to fulfill that goal. For me, Jesus is Lord.

Black youths become skeptical when white people talk about God because many whites are viewed as the same ones who own and support "the system" with its institutions of racism and dehumanization. Black people who talk about God often are one of two types. On one end of the spectrum is the very passive black religious person who is waiting to die and flee the struggles of this life; on the other end is the politically radical black person who believes that worship involves economics and politics. Black models who believe in Jesus Christ and love Him enough to lay down their lives for a brother or sister are difficult to find. This type of model, in seeking to be obedient only to the voice of God, is often called to challenge the political system and the culture of which he or she is a part.

But being an active person in society is not enough, because all believers must confront the struggles of living. Being a spiritual person does not exempt anyone from suffering or from the need to continue to seek God.

I have written this book to tell you of my journey, a journey of learning of His love while finding my call. My awareness of the call began twenty-three years ago and it continues to grow as I follow God. This is not another book that relates only how black people have been mistreated in America. Neither is this a book about political liberation. We really do need a liberation experience, but only God can liberate us! He has liberated me from much of my imprisonment, and I am confident that He will continue to liberate me until I am totally free. He wants you to be free too.

On this journey of mine, I have found great joy and great sorrow. There have been many victories and many defeats. I now have a few answers, but there are still many questions. There are days when it is difficult to wait for the God of my life to speak, but perhaps it is the way we approach the journey and follow our commitment to Him that matters most. It is important to know that although the road may not always be lit with sunshine, the clouds don't last forever either.

Lordship is closely related to slavery. But unlike the slavery imposed upon blacks, or the slavery of many whites to power and money, true lordship—the lordship of Christ—sets us free. Many blacks will wonder why I speak in this book about loving whites and forgiving them. Many whites will want to know why I have not been more positive about their political system. Both blacks and whites must understand that this book is about *my* search for truth. I share this story to offer hope to others who also are searching.

This book has not been easy to write. I have agonized over many points because I wanted to communicate the best I could. Many restless and sleepless nights of prayer were spent as I recalled the experiences that I now want to share with you. My prayer is simply that God will bless you and that you will listen for His special call for your life. You, my friend, are very unique, and the family of God needs your obedient service. Be blessed always.

Cathy Meeks
Macon, Georgia

Chapter 1

To Be Like Him

"I wish I could have a day off." Believe me, that was a prayer I said the day the judge yelled at me on the telephone.

The problem that led to my stormy conversation with the judge had begun three weeks earlier when a friend and I went to file a complaint at the civil court office. During our visit we had been treated very rudely by several people. In addition to the discourtesy shown us in the court clerk's office, we had witnessed the disrespectful treatment of several black laborers. My friend and I were crushed by the manners and attitudes displayed. I became angry enough to make a verbal complaint regarding the matter.

My first stop was at the county sheriff's office where I received very patronizing treatment. The sheriff and his secretary made me nervous with the "super courtesy." Somehow I felt the rudeness in the court clerk's office had been more honest. At any rate, the sheriff was greatly relieved to learn that his office was not responsible for our mistreatment and he apologized for those who had been rude. I told him that there was no excuse for public servants who behaved the way these people had. The sheriff didn't respond, but quickly suggested I talk to the civil court judge about my complaint.

I went again to the civil court clerk's office and asked what time the judge would be in his office. The woman standing behind the desk glared at me as she said "There are some chairs around the corner, go around there and wait."

I told her that I didn't have time to wait and asked if I could make an appointment to see the judge later. "No!" she snapped.

"Is there a secretary whom I can talk with about making an appointment?" I asked. She did not answer, but instead turned and yelled for another woman to come and help.

The second woman proved to be even more angry than the first. It was only 9:15 A.M., but she already looked tired. She grunted at me and mumbled something. The part of her mumble

I understood indicated that I should follow her. We walked down the hall to another office—which I learned belonged to the judge.

My escort asked, "Why do you want to see the judge?"

"It regards a situation that has to do with filing a complaint," I answered.

"What was the complaint?"

"It concerns the way a friend and I were treated, but I want to discuss this with the judge."

The lady became very defensive and started yelling at me in an enraged voice. I said as calmly as I could, "I just want to make an appointment with the judge and discuss this matter with him." The clerk took my name and instructed me to call the judge. I thanked her and left.

By the time I returned to my office at Mercer University, I was very frustrated. The meetings and appointments of the morning were not enough to keep my mind from my encounter at the county courthouse.

Later that day, I called the judge as his secretary had told me to do. He had already talked with several people in the civil court office and had determined that we had been treated courteously.

Immediately, the judge started shouting at me, accusing me of making false accusations and of having a chip on my shoulder. "You should come down here and talk to these people," he said. "They don't remember being rude to you. You are trying to start trouble."

"No sir, I am not. I just believe that someone needs to say something about what is going on in some of the offices that serve the citizens," I answered. Deep in my heart I was praying, "Lord, please help me to be kind to this man and not become defensive."

"You know all of these people go to church and to Oral Roberts's campaigns and they are good people," the judge said angrily.

"I am in no way saying that they are not good: I am simply saying that they treated my friend and me rudely and that there is no excuse for that," I answered. "Judge, I really would like to come to your office and discuss this matter; I don't like talking about things like this on the phone."

He then became even more angry, and at the top of his voice told me that he wasn't going to waste his time talking to me. He accused me of being upset with his ruling in my friend's case. He was mistaken. My irritation had nothing to do with the court ruling; besides, I would have ruled as he did based on the information presented to him that day in court. He referred me to another man and made it clear that he didn't want to talk to me any more. I thanked him and said goodbye.

I sat at my desk and prayed, "Lord, it is too hard to be like You. I get so tired of trying to love and accept people like the judge, the sheriff, and the secretary. I get tired of being black and sensitive to the plight of other blacks and poor people. I wish I could have a day off."

But there are no days off when you are trying to live in response to the call to be like Him. There is hope, though, because you know He will not leave you. I am thankful that when I was young Jesus called me to be like Him.. He put the desire in my heart and gave me the courage to start the journey. And he has helped strengthen that desire as I have confronted the various situations of life that have forced me to decide whether I wanted to be like him or to seek some other way.

For example, in responding to that judge, Jesus wanted me to be calm and loving—not angry and hostile. That was not easy, and without the help of a loving Father, it would have been impossible. On days like the one I just described, I wonder if there might not be another way. Perhaps, if I tried, I could find something easier. But then as I ask with the disciples of long ago, "To whom shall I go?" I know there is no other.

Jesus made it clear that "taking up my cross and following Him" includes being reconciled to the oneness of all believers. Neither you nor I have a choice in the matter if we are seeking to be like Him. He does not ask us to think of ways to be partially like Him, or to negotiate the way that we like best. We have no choice in the matter; He expects us to be like Him.

After we decide to accept His call, we lose our chance to choose because to choose anything other than being changed into His likeness would be far too painful. Of course, the process of being changed is painful too. Maybe it is simply a choice between more pain or less pain.

Somehow, it always seems that obedience results in less pain than disobedience. Because of this truth and our efforts to show that we love Jesus and His Father, our behavior should be changed. There is no way we can say that God is important in our lives and yet continue to live without seeking who and what He wants us to be. Once we have made that discovery for ourselves, then we need to get on with the business of allowing the Holy Spirit to reshape us.

Why do so many churches fail to acknowledge that there is a Lord to be like? In our little church in Arkansas, I can remember very little teaching about Jesus and none about how He related to the daily process of living. Later, when I went to college, I hoped I would find churches teaching how a deeper awareness of Jesus related to living, but that was not the case. Little was said about being changed, because most folks seemed to be too busy being conformists to talk about being different.

I understand how people feel who want to keep things just as they are. Life would be easier if we could just get Jesus to be Who and What we would like Him to be. But if He is to be the potter and we the clay, we have to give up so very much. It is hard not to want to be the potter ourselves.

My anger and disappointment with the black church arise from this very issue. It has created a Jesus of its own. Of course, the white church has done this also, but the irony of it is that the Jesus created by both churches is almost identical.

God has been made to be a mere "force" (like that in the movie *Star Wars*) who is asked to approve of the programs and projects the church wants. The black church remained quiet for a long time on most issues. It made efforts to meet the social needs of its members, but the spiritual needs were not dealt with. There was a cultural and emotional commitment to religion, but being a Christian was—and still is—a cultural endeavor for many black people. The result was that whatever went on in the culture was practiced and supported by the church.

During the 1950s and 1960s, we heard a great deal about a theology of liberation. Unquestionably, somebody needed to talk about being liberated, but to allow liberation to become the essence of the journey was sad. Today we are paying a high price in the black community for this kind of theology. Black people have lost hope and a feeling of identity with the only One who can offer them stability.

A theology that makes Jesus into a black man with an Afro misses the point just as surely as the theology which makes Jesus blue-eyed and blond. *It is not a matter of making Him like us; we are to become like Him.*

I do understand the need to have a God with whom we can identify. However, I believe the way to seek Him is not through a new theology, but by asking who God is, where He is, what He is, and what the answers to these questions have to do with me. Although we need to search for truth about Him everywhere we can, it is essential that we search with the heart of a genuine seeker of truth and not as one having all the answers.

He is the potter and He is in the business of molding. If we will become like clay and permit Him to mold us, we can find answers to our questions.

Another problem people in general—black people in particular —have is that we feel as if we have a right to a better life—a life of affluence and security. We have bought the "American Dream" and all of its middle-class values. We believe the myths of our culture. Black folks who strive so hard to get their piece of the pie need to be reminded that there is no pie for them. We need to remember that when we set up the "American Dream" as our standard, we leave ourselves open to disillusionment and hostility.

The media surely have not lessened this problem of false hope either. We are wrapped up in television, radio, movies, magazines, and all the other propaganda devices of our culture, and a sickness results because we believe what we see and hear.

We are told happiness comes if you are a success and have all the right gadgets. Success will probably result if you play your cards right, and the gadgets can be bought at the nearest shopping center.

In the black community we have the questionable fortune of having magazines like *Ebony*. This magazine, published by a black publisher and distributed to a large number of blacks, chooses to reflect only the values of the "Dream." A friend has accused me of wanting *Ebony* to be a Christian magazine. This is not the case.

However, I do wish this publication would stop printing articles about people who own eight Rolls Royces or telling how many furs so-and-so has. I wish *Ebony* would forget the stories about people who are already famous and instead tell its audience that there is something more to life than clothes, cars, houses, and food.

Another image that has emerged in the print media recently is that of the black who does as much as possible to be white. To be O.K., a black has to have light skin and straight hair. It reminds me of those days in the 1950s when we bleached our faces and pressed our hair with hot combs or chemicals. Remember how we got away from some of that in the 1960s because we were busy saying "I am black and I am proud"? I can't help wondering where the pride has gone.

Let me make it clear that I don't care whether or not a person has straight hair. But I do care about why their hair is straightened and whether or not it's being done because they can't deal with who they are. That is cause for concern.

Today it is advantageous to be black (if you can manage not to be too black) because the laws have forced most institutions to have a "token." If you can fit in without bringing too much attention to yourself, you can really go places. You see, the black media tell us these myths are true. The white media talk about what it is like to be white and so do the black media. My point is simply that as long as we have the type of black models presented in television shows like "The Jeffersons," "Sanford and Son," "Good Times," and "That's My Mama," we are in trouble.

Think of the characters in these programs; they are all recreations of the "Amos and Andy" characters. For instance, Sapphire, the wife of Kingfish in "Amos and Andy," was presented as being smarter than her husband. She was always getting him out of the trouble that he was too stupid to get out of by himself. So who wants to be like the idiot Kingfish or the con-artist Fred Sanford? For that matter, who wants to be like Sapphire? The images are sick, and when we pattern our lives and our values after them, we become sick as well.

The horrifying fact is that the church, too, permits the media to dictate its identity. It should be the other way around. No wonder so many people who have tried to participate in the religious activities of the church feel there is no difference between those activities and the culture in general. They are right; there is no difference.

I can remember how Plato's *Allegory of the Cave* impressed me when I read if for the first time. He describes a person who lives in a cave and is chained so he cannot move. Images are reflected on the wall, but the images are not of anything real; they are of other images. The chained person doesn't know this; he thinks the images are real. His whole view of reality is based on something that is not real.

Plato's allegory gives us a good description of our culture and our church. The only difference is that there is a way for us to take the chains off, because if we will we can turn away from the images and their myths. We can know what reality is if we want to. Life can be lived in another dimension.

A person interested in leaving the way of the crowd and accepting the challenge "to come and follow me" must break some of the ties with man-made tradition. Many church people are more committed to tradition than they have ever been to the Lord. The traditions help us to be merely "cultural Christians." For example, in the black church, there is the tradition of responding orally to the minister. In addition, a lot of emotionalism is encouraged.

The result is that many people go to worship services Sunday after Sunday and their spirits are never really touched nor their lives changed. After all of the emotional dramatizing has ended and people have shouted and cried, the struggles of reality—which could be made easier by a dimension of true spirituality—still have to be confronted.

I remember hearing many radical speeches in the 1960s on many topics. I can even remember a few preachers talking about radicalism in the faith. I don't know what those pastors meant, but I am sure as I sit here writing today that their notions and mine were not the same of the issue of being a radical Christian.

I think Jesus was a radical person in the truest sense. He refused to support the religious establishment and he refused to choose safe roads to travel. I am still appalled at how easily I choose the safe road and how much I resist taking a stand on issues that threaten my security. However, through His grace there have been times when I have received the courage to make radical choices (like the complaint to the judge). But always there has been a good bit of agony.

So many of us are captivated by our affluence. We accept comfort as though it were a right rather than a gift. As one who lived the first twenty-five years of her life with barely enough material goods to survive, I am grateful that God has graciously helped me enter the struggle which I trust will make me a truly radical Christian. The journey thus far has not been easy, but I want to share some of it with you in the pages of this book.

Chapter 2

Seeking the Way

My story is not unlike that of hundreds of other blacks in this land. The distinguishing factor between mine and theirs is that God has decided that my story should be told. My life has been and continues to be very ordinary and simple.

It all began in a sleepy little place called Junction City, a town claimed by both Arkansas and Louisiana. When we lived there, Junction City had a population of two hundred. Because it had few employment opportunities—with the exception of a lumber mill—people who wanted a job were forced to migrate sixteen miles to the city of Eldorado. There my mother's family lived on a little plot of land my grandfather had homesteaded many years earlier.

My father had been married before. After he and my mother were married, they moved into the old rat-infested house on my grandfather's land. (Daddy and his family had no land.) Several of the seven children from his previous marriage moved in with them because their mother had died when they were very young. Because my daddy was twenty years older than my mother, some of the children from his first marriage were almost as old as their new stepmother.

We lived in that house until I was five years old, and then my family moved to Moro, Arkansas, another sleepy little town of 189 people.

Although Mama had no degree, she got a job teaching in an all black school there. This was possible because the white school boards did not require black teachers in black schools to be as well trained as white teachers in white schools had to be.

My daddy had no promise of a job, but he hoped to find a farm on which he could sharecrop. Sharecropping—even today—means that you work for a white landowner and split the profits with him. Because you have no money when you begin the agreement, you must borrow for the year to come. At the end of the first year, you pay the landowner back from your profits—but you must borrow again to get through the next year. Under the system, you almost never get out of debt, nor do you get into a position to own land yourself.

Daddy was a sharecropper until his death in 1962, and, as you might expect, we were a very poor family.

Daddy's education ended after the third or fourth grade. He did not testify about being a Christian, and there were times when he was not even a good man. At times, the pain of being black and poor was more than he could bear. If you have not lived in poverty, then the plight of my family will be difficult for you to understand. But I do want to try to explain what it was like.

Often my father became very hostile toward us, the people closest to him. I suppose we were the only ones he dared show how he really felt about life. Unfortunately, we were not able to understand his behavior and it caused all of us much anguish.

My daddy learned at an early age what every black person learns in this country: the only thing worse than a "nigger" is a "smart nigger."

A "smart nigger" is a person who dares to stand up for his rights and tries to maintain a little dignity for himself. Black males in particular must avoid being "smart." If a black man wants to live with a minimum of hassles from white folk, he learns to take a lot of abuse without saying anything. My daddy learned this lesson well—maybe too well.

As Daddy tried to find ways to have a little dignity—something every person needs in order to survive—and yet not to be a "smart nigger," he became an awfully hard person to live with. He had high blood pressure, was always depressed, and he had migraine headaches that forced him to spend hours at a time in bed.

I can't even begin to imagine what life must have been like for him. He never had any real security. He was always a share-cropper because he never owned any land. As a matter of fact, he never owned anything.

Sharecropping is merely a glorified version of slavery. It is designed to keep people dependent and in bondage. Do you remember the plight of the laborer in Tennessee Ernie Ford's old song "Sixteen Tons"? My daddy never did work himself out of his obligation to the company store.

In the spring we always owed money for the food we had bought on credit during the previous winter. At the end of the harvest there were the bills for seed, fertilizer, and supplies. There was no way to ever get out of debt. Somehow the money Mama earned teaching school didn't seem to help. Maybe it was because her salary was so small.

Some of my earliest memories of sorrow are connected with seeing my father come home after the settlement with the landowner. His face had such a sad look. He walked as if his feet weighed too much for him to pick up.

Always in debt, my parents taught us as we grew up that the only way poor folks could have anything was to buy on credit. They considered debt to be as much a part of life as breathing. They expected to owe people money until the day they died. My daddy was right; he died and left all kinds of debts for us to pay.

Daddy had a stroke in November, 1962, and died at age seventy. At least that was the official date of his death; but reflection upon his life makes me wonder if he hadn't died many years previously. Perhaps he died in the year he started to believe that he had no hope of a better life. You see, Daddy had lost hope for himself and for us. A person without hope is dangerous. He hurts others or himself—or both.

Even though the rest of us in the family had our whole lives to live, Daddy usually avoided anything that would have involved him with life. He often told us we would fail at some project we were about to undertake. For example, when I was in the seventh grade, one of my teachers asked me to memorize Edgar Allan Poe's *The Raven*. My daddy didn't want me even to try to learn it. He didn't think I could. His objections were hard to understand and they hurt me and made me angry. I just thought he was trying to be difficult. I became determined to prove to him that I could do something besides chop and pick cotton. I learned *The Raven* and recited it without a mistake.

Today as I reflect on my daddy's behavior, I understand that he was afraid for us. He didn't want us to be hurt and disillusioned the way he had been. I wish I had known this back then; it would have made a difference between us.

There are two things I want to make very clear. One of them is that I will always be grateful that my daddy had the courage not to leave my family until his death. I don't know why he stayed, but he did and I am glad. The second thing I want known is that all young poor people—and black people in particular—need to be aware that parents often discourage their children because they are afraid. They desire so much for their children to have what they themselves have missed, but their sense of reality makes them wonder if it is ever possible. Thus, they express their fear and doubt by being negative. If your parents are like this, be patient and understanding with them.

My family of six lived like sardines in that three room house for the first six years we lived in Moro. The old place left much to be desired. It had cracks, and the rats knew where they were. The presence and boldness of the rats was often revealed by the droppings and stains on the old newspapers that lined the bottom of our dresser drawers. Often they would chew holes in our clothes and seemed always to choose my most valuable items, such as my one bra or my one good slip. The rats chewed holes in both.

My two sisters, my brother, and I slept in the same room. In the winter we all slept in the same bed so we could stay warm. I can remember how I came to wish for my own room—a place of my own where I could keep my things and have some privacy. My brother always seemed to find my little secrets and then I would be forced to bribe him with part of my food so that he wouldn't tell Mama and Daddy about my "love letters" or other private matters. Those letters were never to be mailed anyway, because they were only my fantasies. But they were mine and I didn't want to share them with anyone.

I could bribe my brother with food because it was the only thing I felt that he wanted. Food was very significant at our house, probably because we never had much of it. Daddy used to place a lot of emphasis on our ability to eat large amounts of food.

Being able to eat food in large quantities was considered a sign of good health, but the result was terrible for me. I developed a weight problem, and by the time I was fifteen, my weight had soared to 185 pounds. It didn't matter to my family that I was beginning to resemble "Porky the Pig"; they continued to encourage me to eat meals consisting of half a dozen biscuits, fried potatoes, and sugar syrup (made from sugar and water). Daddy was very pleased when we ate all of the food Mama had cooked. In my efforts to please him, I ate too much.

Our diet consisted mainly of biscuits, cornbread, potatoes, brown gravy, mackerel, and sugar syrup. Vegetables and fruit were rarely on our table. I remember the delight that used to fill my heart whenever I could get an apple. It wasn't often so it tasted even better—kind of like a cold glass of lemonade on a hot day.

I loved summer because for a few months we would have all the vegetables we could eat from our garden. Tomatoes, pulled from the vine and eaten with salt, tasted so good. Something in my body seemed to crave vegetables, and I would eat them even at breakfast almost every day during the spring and summer months.

Oh, how much a plate of greens and bread means to me! Most of the time, a meal of fried chicken, biscuits, gravy, and orange juice was the best breakfast we could have—except during the spring and summer when we had greens. In the springtime, I would go to the garden and pick those tiny little mustard leaves. Because they were usually filled with dirt and sometimes had lice, they had to be washed many times. I would pump water from our rusty old handpump until they were clean and ready to cook. The sweet fragrance from my prize pot of greens would fill the entire house. Even though the rest of my family had eaten breakfast hours before my greens were ready, that was all right with me. Often it was almost noon before I sat down to eat my prized plate of greens and cornbread. What a treat they were!

Along with my family's food shortage was a clothing shortage. I always felt inferior because my clothes never looked good. Not only was I fat, but I also had big feet. I thought I was the ugliest person around.

One of my more vivid childhood memories is that I always missed the first day if school because I never had shoes. I don't really know why, but for some reason my parents never bought shoes for me until after school had started.

Missing the first day of school was a sad affair for me. Each year we were dismissed from school in May so that we could work in the fields until July. This "split term" was used because so many of us were from farm families. During the summer we worked in the fields and never saw any of our friends until school reopened. The first day back at school was a time of reunion. It was so exciting that I used to lie awake at night and pray that I wouldn't miss opening day. But I did. I always did.

My mother, sisters, and brother would go to school and leave me home with Daddy. I would be angry and cry. Daddy would promise to get my shoes "pretty soon." I would start hoping I could go to school in a couple of days. Besides seeing my friends, I really liked school itself. It was my only contact with a world that differed from the crowded, burden-filled one I shared at home with my family.

Another memory of the hard times of my childhood is the fear that I had that my parents would be taken away by bill collectors. Since we had no telephone, the collectors came directly to our house. I was always afraid they would put my folks in jail. I am grateful they never did.

Most of my family memories relate to hard times. The winters were always the worst. Not only did we have a poor diet, we sometimes had no food at all. There were also times when we had no fuel, and to cook bread we had to make a fire outside. To keep from freezing indoors we crowded near a little electric heater and wrapped up in quilts. In those times I learned a lot about fear. The fear of starvation, freezing to death, or being left without parents constantly haunted me even in the best of times.

It wasn't until years later that I realized how some of that childhood fear had carried over into my adulthood. I became aware of a constant concern with food. I knew I had adequate resources to buy whatever food I needed, but I always worried about having enough. Food was always on my mind and I was hungry most of the time. My weight was constantly rising and I was getting depressed.

Because of God's unrelenting efforts to provide total healing for me, I have been able to come to terms with these old fears. Even though my refrigerator and cupboards are emptier these days, I always have enough food. I have lost over forty pounds and I feel certain that I am on my way to a more normal weight. I am thankful for the wholeness, for the release from past fears, that continues to come to me each day through the power of the Holy Spirit. God is truly merciful and faithful!

The awareness of those childhood fears has helped me to face other areas of my life that need healing. This has been particularly true in regard to how I view the gifts God allows me to have.

My black, rural lifestyle had taught me that being in debt was the only possible way to live—even though I naturally wanted all of the pretty things I had never owned before.

Let me explain how my early years of poverty and want affected the way I was to live as an adult. I believe these attitudes and values tell me where I especially need to rely on Jesus Christ.

After getting my first full-time job, I rushed to take my place in our good old consumer society. I filled my wallet with credit cards and started out to buy comfort and a sense of well-being.

It took the jolting experience of charging all of my cards to the credit limit to make me realize that real comfort and security can't be bought with Master Charge. With the power of the Holy Spirit, I have since been able to choose to live without credit cards.

Not everyone will be as extreme in their use of credit cards as I was, but using credit can become a dangerous habit. Do you ever wonder what the scripture means that says "owe no man"? I do.

As a result of not having charge cards, I have had to become more creative. Recently, I bought some sturdy old furniture and refinished it. It was cheap, but it looks great. And the best thing of all is that it's paid for.

As a believer in Christ, I am called to live a more simple life. Remember how Jesus said that foxes have holes, but the Son Of Man has no place to lay His head? Remember the quarters where He was born? This helps me to have clues about what my lifestyle should be.

The problem with a complex life, one that demands so many conveniences and gadgets, is that it requires too much money and too many resources. There is never enough to get everything we want or think that we need.

I find there is always something else I want. It may be another item for the house, a new dress, or another shade of nail polish. I have had to struggle prayerfully to establish priorities for my needs and wants. There are times when I think I must have something, but if I will wait a few days, I often find that I can live without it.

I believe with all my heart that any person who knows and loves Jesus must deal with the question, "What does it mean to follow Him?" I feel an honest evaluation will lead to the conclusion that as followers of Christ we must be something other than a reflection of our culture. No Christian is allowed to choose his or her own way. Race, sex, or marital status does not excuse anyone from being radical in the journey with the Lord Jesus.

All of the things we have received from the hands of a gracious and loving Father are to be shared—and in many instances —given away completely. As I have tried to incorporate this truth into my life and style of living, the Lord has called on me to share my possessions in all kinds of ways.

Food—the types I eat and how much of it I share with my friends—is one of the areas I have had to rethink. I am learning to conserve food by shopping more carefully and learning how to substitute protein substances for meat. I cook a lot of peas, beans, and lentils these days. I eat more cheese, cottage cheese, and eggs. I eat less at meals and am learning to skip some meals. There is no reason why one person should eat three or four times a day when other people in our world have nothing at all to eat. I am finding there are ways to share the money I save on food with those who have neither food nor money.

These experiences have also led me to a decision on tithing. I used to think I would tithe whenever all of my bills were paid. God had another notion. The long steady conflict lasted about two years, but finally I was ready to do it. I committed ten percent of my paycheck to the Lord and His work in the world. God has blessed me since then. No, I have not received bundles of extra money, but He always provides for my needs just as He did before I began to tithe. After all, His love is not given to me as a result of what I do.

Hopefully, someday I will be able to give half of my salary away. I just don't believe I have the right to spend as much money as possible on myself. I believe God has blessed me—not because He wants me to become a more effective consumer—but rather because He wants me to help somebody.

Trying to live a simpler life is not easy. I struggle with it every day as I try to establish priorities in my life. I carefully consider things like what books to read, how to use my time, which new responsibilities of service to take on, or even how to rest and relax. There will always be tension in trying to live a balanced life and trying to stay focused on the only One who can give us the proper perspective.

It is the responsibility of each person to examine his or her own personal life and look for ways to structure simplicity into it. Perhaps the first thing that has to happen is the realization of a need for change. After that, the needed courage and grace have to be sought from the Lord.

I have to ask God constantly to help me achieve my top priority of living differently. I have to set aside time for quietness, or as the fathers of the ancient church called it, "contemplation." This means some chores are left undone, but I am usually able to finish most of the essential ones. Changing a life takes a lot of redirecting of the will and practice at discipline.

As a black person, I have had to accept the fact that Jesus wants me to accept His call just like anybody else. Having been poverty-stricken as a child is no excuse! I do have wounds caused by the poverty of my earlier years, and they will probably always cause me suffering. But God has used some of those injuries to help me become more sensitive and more concerned about the poverty of others.

There is nothing glamorous about poverty, but it can serve as a creative force in one's life. I am thankful to God that He has used the poverty of my life in this way. Perhaps it is harder for poor people or black people to accept the call to live a life of simplicity, but He never calls us to do anything without giving us the grace to do it.

For a long time I wanted to be affluent. It was always the one dream that all of us in my family had. I wanted to have many pretty clothes. But I have learned I can be a very attractive person without spending my entire income on clothes. I have learned to sew, to watch for sales, and to use my creativity in putting my wardrobe together.

Now, since I realize that I really am the daughter of a King and as a princess have no business looking tacky while representing my Father, I can relax and use my creativity to make my wardrobe adequate. I am always amazed when someone comments about how good something looks that I am wearing and I realize the whole outfit cost less than ten dollars.

Yes, we have been called to a new way of living. The joyous truth is that Jesus stands ready to give us all the gifts we need to make the journey.

Chapter 3

Dreamers

I've always trusted my younger brother William. When he became old enough to drive, I felt safer riding with him than I did with Mama or Daddy. I would follow him anywhere. He always took me fishing with him, but I don't know why he wanted to bother with me. I was afraid of everything—the bait, the water, and the fish after they were caught.

On one of our fishing trips, we needed to cross to the other side of the fishing pond where the fish were biting better. This was my brother's idea, naturally, and a dumb one, since the only way to get there was to wade across. Well, I agreed to let him carry me across on his back. As you already know, I wasn't exactly light as a feather in those days and so this was no small accomplishment. We slipped and slopped along, and much to my surprise, we made it across. It was a good thing the water was shallow or my brother might still be stuck in the bottom of that pond!

When we had started wading I didn't know how deep the water was, but I trusted him. He said we would be O.K. and I believed him. He was usually right. Sometimes he got us into tight spots, but he always managed to find a way out.

My brother has always been a very creative and imaginative person. He likes to work with his hands and can build anything. He hated school, and because the teachers never made any effort to meet him where he was, he stumbled through high school and graduated in time to be drafted for military service in Vietnam. The day he left for Vietnam was the saddest day I can remember; I thought I would never see him alive again. Thankfully, a year later he came home.

When we were kids, my brother made all kinds of toys for us to play with. Although we didn't have much time to play in the summer because of the field work, we made up for lost time during the winter. He made cars, paper money, and houses out of boxes—and we dreamed of traveling to any faraway place we could think of.

Much of our play was an enactment of our daydreams. Oftentimes this is true for black children because they own nothing but dreams. We dreamed about a better day, a day when we would have decent clothes, more food, and a house that didn't leak or have rats. That was our constant fantasy. We had no way of knowing how many years were to pass before those dreams would come true. It is probably a good thing we didn't know.

"Dreamer" is the single word I would choose to describe all of us in my family during those early years. Dreamers we surely were, and maybe God used our dreams to save our lives. We always talked about a better day. We kept hoping. We believed.

Perhaps it is this same unwillingness to be crushed by the despair of reality that can be seen in black children of today. Because they have such great odds to overcome in order to make it in life, many of them end up playing "Superfly." We want to condemn them because "Superfly" is a pimp. But they have no idea what a pimp is; they just want somebody to know their names.

If the pimp and the con-artist are the models we present to black youth, then they will have only them to dream about. Black youth merely want to find ways to face their world, and hope for a better day is actually a healthy way of facing misery.

Because children are so sensitive and have such deep impressions made upon them by all kinds of things, it is important that we assume some responsibility for providing them with proper emotional and intellectual food.

I was blessed to have an aunt who took it upon herself to help provide for my intellectual and emotional feeding. It made a difference in my dreams and daydreams.

As a child, daydreaming almost became a way of life for me. I daydreamed about getting away and about Daddy changing. But daydreams are like sunrises; sooner or later the brightness makes you realize that your world is not the one you were dreaming of.

Escaping is not easy when you have nowhere to go, but I tried, mostly through reading and listening to the radio. I would talk Daddy into getting a newspaper and would read every column inch of it. I listened to the news on the radio, and Lowell Thomas and Edward R. Murrow became close friends of mine. I remember when the crisis in the Congo in 1960 caused the United Nations

General Assembly to go into emergency session. I listened to the sessions on the radio. Hearing about the outside world gave me hope.

We had a little brown radio that picked up every station in Arkansas and half of the ones in Tennessee. It sat on an old brown chest of drawers that had the paint peeling off. I didn't even mind the static on the radio because it gave me a chance to hear the Metropolitan Opera Company and the New York Philharmonic Orchestra. The music made me feel as if I were a part of a better world. I listened faithfully every Saturday even though I didn't understand half of the music or the words in the operas.

Before the radio concerts began, I would get my old split-bottom chair (which had been made by Grandpa from white oak trees) and put my sister Irene in my lap. Then as I rocked her, I would listen to my programs and cry.

Irene was born when I was eight years old and I took care of her much of the time. While we worked in the fields, I watched her in her crib. I would play with her until she fell asleep; then I would chop cotton until she awoke. I stayed home from school with her when she was sick. In effect I became her mother, which was unfortunate for both of us. I needed somebody to love, and she was that somebody. It seems as if little children love you without attaching strings. My little sister loved me that way and I really needed it.

In later years we had to pay a high price in suffering for this relationship, but at the time it met needs for both of us which might not have been met otherwise. Besides, we are both aware of these problems now and have worked through many of them. Maybe that initial love for each other has given us the strength and courage to accomplish this.

Holding her in my lap and rocking her provided a sense of security for me—especially during those times when Daddy threatened to take the radio away from me. My family didn't understand me. They just couldn't understand why anybody would want to listen to all of that classical music and opera.

My reason for reading and listening to the music was simple: I was rebelling against being forced to live in the world of my family. I wanted to get away from it. Several nights a week I would cry myself to sleep, but the tears didn't relieve the anguish in my soul. I am thankful now to the Father that suffering is not a terminal condition.

As I grew older, I started to shut myself off from my family. I lost myself in work: cooking, taking care of my sister, cleaning the house, washing and ironing clothes. My day of housework would start about 6:30 in the morning and end around 9:30 at night.

My sister Lena hated housework and so she welcomed my undying weekly efforts to find healing by working myself half to death. Lena is a physically beautiful person. For one thing she is skinny, a fact which always made me jealous. She has the beautiful kind of hair that makes a fantastic Afro and her skin is smooth and free of pimples.

Lena is also quite intelligent. She excelled in mathematics, but when it was time to work, she preferred the yard and garden to the house. Her preference caused us a few problems when we lived together. We played together as children but were never close. If you have a sister like that, you know what it's like.

Our lives took very different directions and over the years the distance between us widened instead of narrowed. Recently, though, we've started to see each other's personal worth and to accept one another. That acceptance has led us to a deep respect and a new friendship.

"Dreamer" is also a word that can be used to describe my mother. Mama was a part-time college student for eighteen years. She finally graduated with a B.A. in education the same year I finished high school. She had refused to believe she couldn't make it. She took correspondence courses, taught school, worked in the fields, and cared for us. She caught rides to night classes with my uncle in his old beige Chevrolet or rode with anyone else who was taking classes with her. She was fifty-three years old when she received her degree.

At age fifty-nine, Mama became the victim of "social progress" —as so many black and poor people do. She was fired from her teaching job in Wheately, Arkansas because the school system there had a surplus of black teachers after integration.

After losing her job, my mother was discovered by a recruiter of teachers from Bakersfield, California, and was hired to teach there. She later sued the school district in Arkansas and won all of her back salary plus her moving expenses to the West Coast. I think it was during this time that I started to be suspicious of social progress.

Because there were dreamers around me, I managed to survive and find ways to cope with my insecure and confusing world. One of the ways I coped was by reading some Bible storybooks an aunt gave to my family. I read them again and again. Our old, dusty, worn, and mite-filled King James Bible also kept making my list of books to read. I read the Gospels even though I probably didn't know at the time what they were called; I simply liked to read about Jesus. He seemed to be a special person and I thought about Him a lot. Sometimes, early in the morning while the rest of my family still slept, I would get up, go to the back door steps, and sit and think about Him. Maybe it was there that I first began to hear the knocking on my heart's door from the One who would later enter as the lovely Guest.

It was always a special treat to sit on the back door steps watching the sunrise and smelling the freshness of the dew-dampened air mingled with the sweetness of the honey-suckle. Somehow I felt comforted by the songs of the birds and the fact that the sun kept rising in the sky.

I would feel a strong urge to know more about the rest of the world. I felt as if I belonged some place else—not on that farm. There was something in me screaming, "get away!" But I didn't know where I was to go. Who would tell me?

So I kept talking to Jesus and reading about Him. I thought about all the miracles He had performed and I wondered if He could do any miracles for my family and me. I asked Him for rain and for my daddy to make a lot of cotton. And I always asked Him for food.

Some days, as I sat on those splintery back steps, which had been whitened by the cold winter rains and probably by other tears of anguish just like mine, my eyes would turn to the bright pretty colors in the sky. My mind would wonder why the warmth of the beautiful morning sun couldn't warm my heart and make my world better. But wondering didn't seem to help.

Members of my family did not talk about feelings and it became increasingly easy to live in my own silence. Unknowingly, Daddy helped me keep to myself by buying a T.V. set from Sears.

The T.V. was the worst thing that could have ever happened to us because my sisters, brothers, and I stopped playing together. We lost much of our creativity because we just had to push a button for entertainment.

You may wonder why my daddy bought a T.V. set when we didn't have enough fuel or food. The answer is simple: it is difficult to defer material gratification when you have little or nothing. Viewing an old black and white set while you wait for enough money to buy a color T.V. is not nearly as tough as waiting to buy a T.V. at all.

My daddy knew that we couldn't afford a T.V., but he wanted us to have it and the only way he could get it was on the Sears easy payment plan.

When I worked at the Memphis Board of Education, some of my colleagues were critical of the welfare recipients who had color T.V.'s and old Cadillacs. That's not my notion of setting proper priorities either, but I understand how deep the needs for fulfillment go. When people don't have anything, they get the things that will help them best forget that they have nothing.

It makes me want to cry when I see a young black man wearing a cheap suit and cheap cut glass rings on his fingers. I know that he feels security can be bought at the local pawn shop. He's just like the welfare mother who gets ripped-off by the local furniture dealer. How many times have I seen those cheap velvet living room sets in the homes of welfare mothers? I knew they had paid two or three times what they were worth, but credit was all they had and they bought with it what they could.

Perhaps the greatest plight of the poverty stricken is that they become victims of themselves. They are paralyzed by their needs and wants. They have a lot of difficulty trying to set the best priorities for themselves and in finding the courage to discipline themselves enough to reach their goals.

But then why should a poor family try to have the same goals as a middle class family? They need to have goals that are realistic for them. They need to be encouraged to grow in whatever ways are best for them. Hopefully, their goals will be something more noble than merely becoming better consumers.

When I was thirteen, my parents told me that I should be baptized. Since we hardly ever went to church, their request didn't make much sense to me. But I was glad because I knew Jesus had been baptized and I thought He might like me better if I were too. It was important that He like me, and so I got excited about the chance to be baptized.

We went one hot August night to the New Hope Baptist Church. They were having a revival and I didn't understand what was going on. I just wanted to be baptized. It was very noisy; many people were screaming and carrying on. I thought they must be awfully sad.

Finally, the week of meetings ended and I had the chance to stand up and say I believed in God. At that time, my awareness of God the Father was very limited. It was Jesus to whom I felt attracted and I wanted to talk about Him. But no one said much regarding Him and neither did I. Excitement rose in me because I felt that Jesus would be pleased with me for being baptized as He had been I was also scared!

My brother and sister had decided to be baptized at the same time. Because the New Hope Church had the custom of doing all its baptizing in the fall, we had to wait until a cold November Sunday morning to be baptized in a slimy green pond not far from the church. We didn't talk much about what we were doing, we just did it. I am sure each one of us who was baptized that day has a scary story to tell about how it felt. I remember afterwards how I continued to get up early to pray. I read my Bible a lot. It was good to feel I was more liked by Jesus, but it was to be many years before I realized how much He really did like me!

After the baptism I prayed even harder for God to take care of us. I wanted so much for our lives to be different. God answered my prayers by giving me a little seed of faith. He kept helping us survive through the cold winters and the food shortages, but for several years after my baptism our lives didn't get much better.

After being baptized, Mama took us to church on the Sundays that Daddy gave us the car. Some Sundays he would take the car and leave. On the other Sundays he would fuss about our going to church, but he usually let us go.

It seems that God wanted me to realize at an early age that becoming a Christian did not mean everything was going to turn into a Cinderella-type fairy tale. Life would continue to be real. It would be difficult and there would be defeats as well as victories. I had not received a special miracle package by being baptized. Baptism was simply my reasonable response to His love.

The little church we attended was a typical rural, southern black church. The pastor came to preach two Sundays each month. He had one standard sermon and he preached it every time. People prayed the same prayers every Sunday, and during each service the same ones got "happy" and shouted. It seemed that nobody entered into a permanent life-changing commitment to Jesus.

The worship service was like a circus. Something deep in my stomach hated the noise. I liked the Sundays better when the preacher wasn't there. I suppose that most of the people who came to our church had a great need for a place to be somebody. There were few places like that and no one came around to tell them that in the Lord's eyes, they already were somebody. Their worship "performance" was not necessary to gain respect.

The church services had little depth and they gave me little with which to face my life. There was no emphasis on spiritual things and no real teaching of the Bible. I wanted somebody to talk about Jesus, but the other things were too demanding and He just didn't make anybody's list of priorities. He stayed on my mind, though, even if they didn't talk about Him in the services.

My brother tired of going to church and he started to stay home with Daddy. Still interested, my sister and I joined the choir. We wanted to belong, but unfortunately there was a great emphasis on money and we didn't have any. If you didn't pay your church dues each month, you were looked down upon. I felt badly about not paying and sometimes I was embarrassed.

I began to wonder if there were any place in the world where I could feel safe and wanted. I often felt the church was too closely related to my frustrating farm world. As a matter of fact, it often felt just like that world. Although I couldn't find Jesus at church,

I found that He was still real to me when I sat on the back-door steps and talked to Him.

When I was fifteen years old, my parents let me go to live with my aunt in Junction City, Arkansas. This time away from home was to prove very helpful to me. Before I left, my father became more depressed and irritable than he had ever been before. He and my brother were having a hard time getting along. I left fearing that they might hurt each other.

The new school, new friends, and new challenges were good for me. I could communicate with my aunt a little bit. I had my own room—it was so nice! It was good to be away from Daddy; I had become very angry with him and didn't like him at all.

I spent much of that year just experiencing the healing of God. He was so faithful. My aunt was proud of me and she encouraged me to try new things. I trusted her enough to share my vision of writing a book someday. She was encouraging, even about an idea as wild as that! She even had me start taking music lessons. I began to realize that I didn't like feeling so angry with Daddy and I started asking Jesus and His Father for help. I wasn't even sure that I could be helped, but I wanted to find out. It was worth the prayers at least.

The Lord did help me, and by the end of school year I felt better toward Daddy. When I returned home that summer, I was able to talk to him without screaming. I had been healed a little; the time away from home and the prayers had made a difference. I will be eternally thankful for that summer at home because my daddy died from a stroke six months later.

Daddy's death was very difficult for all of us and particularly for me because I had hoped that he might be different and we could be friends someday. I couldn't believe he was gone. Neither could I believe Mama could take care of us. Daddy could be domineering; Mama had encouraged that behavior in many different ways. Now she seemed at loose ends. I felt the situation called me to seek courage and to try to help out.

Throughout this trauma we were sustained by God's love. There is no way we could have completed the cotton harvest, moved to a town closer to Mama's school, and faced our grief without God's love and strength. He just kept on being faithful,

and even though I didn't think about Him much, I realized sometime later how much He had helped us.

During those sad days, I spent my spare moments holding my
little sister in my lap. That was quite a task because she had grown
considerably. But I would rock her and cry. There was nothing else
to do at night.

Even when there seems to be no reason for breath to keep coming through your nostrils or for the sun to keep rising in the sky,
things do go on. So life went on for us.

Again, there was little talk in our family about feelings. We
talked about Daddy, but we didn't talk about our grief. We didn't
talk about our anger. We couldn't because it was too close. The
church was of no help to us, or at least not to me. Finally one day
I cried out to Jesus for help. He was the only friend I had, and I
needed Him to understand how lonely I felt.

The strong and undying urge in my heart to have my life make
a difference and to flesh out all of those dreams kept me going
through the lonely days of sorrow that followed Daddy's death.

While at Marian Anderson High School in Brinkley, Arkansas,
I received my first glimpse of what the future might hold. The
school was difficult for me because the schedule was more demanding. There were some new subjects such as French and
chemistry which had not been offered at my former school.

I got involved in some school activities without having to fight
with Daddy. I ran for student body president—the first girl to ever
run for that office. I lost the election, but later was chosen to be ed-
itor of the school yearbook. God used this new school, the new
challenges, and the new relationships to bring further healing.

As long as I live, there will be a little pain in my soul when I
think of Daddy. He was a dreamer who had his dream put off one
time too many. And just as Langston Hughes said in *A Dream
Deferred*, "If a dream is deferred for too long, it festers and dries
up like a raisin." I will always feel the pain of Daddy's deferred
dreams.

Do the festers become redemptive? Maybe they cause us to
realize how much we have to depend on God and how miserable
we are without His constant care. I have learned there is a purpose
for the pain.

Chapter 4

Relinquishment

My life seems to have been filled with theological lessons taught to me long before I even had the language to articulate what I had learned.

The part of my journey spent in California was where I began to learn what it means to relinquish. It was there that I had to give up many of my visions and dreams and accept my finiteness and the certainty of my own death. The pain of all this was almost unbearable. But He never calls us to bear a greater burden than He has given us the strength to bear. Doesn't that fill you with joy and hope?

After graduating from high school, I went to California to attend college. I was to live with my half-brother, Thomas, and attend a community college in Los Angeles. The possibility of going to school was exciting.

Only a God of mercy would be kind enough to reveal just one day at a time. How could we stand it if we had to see too far into the future?

I appreciate this one-day-at-a-time revelation because my first year of college was a nightmare. I went to class but had a very hard time keeping up with the assignments. I soon learned that having been third in my graduating class at a rural Arkansas high school was a matter of irrelevance.

I had missed too many essential subjects. I was not even sure I should be in college and I didn't know if I could make it through. My high school training had been hurt by both mediocre instruction and a mediocre curriculum. I had been a senior in high school before I had a literature class. My math background had been equally poor and I had no aptitude for it anyway. My first foreign language class had been in the eleventh grade. It was clear that high school had in no way prepared me for college.

I became depressed again. My brother didn't understand why I wasn't achieving more success. Living with him wasn't working out either.

Nothing seemed to be going right. I looked everywhere, but a job was not to be found for someone like me who had no skills. I finally did work for awhile as a telephone solicitor for a carpet company, but I never got paid. I was desperate. I took another job and that employer paid me with a bad check.

Yes, I was finding out there was more to the world than our little Arkansas farm, and I wasn't sure how I felt about it. I didn't have any friends. I went to school every day and then came home immediately. I was afraid to open my mouth in class for fear of saying something really stupid.

My second semester was an improvement because I enrolled in a speech class. The professor seemed to be really weird, but after hearing me give my first speech, he suggested I join the speech team and sent me to talk to the team's coach.

The coach turned out to be a fairly young man and he seemed quite nice. I was anxious to talk with someone who could reassure me about this whole experience. The coach explained the program and asked me to write a speech on a controversial issue. I chose "Abortion." I thought it was controversial, and I was right. I wrote the speech and he hated it. I rewrote it and he was not impressed. I worked on it some more and finally the speech was polished enough to enter competition.

During all of this, I was experiencing a problem that I did not fully recognize until many years later. I did not know how to relate to white people, nor to men of any color. Here I was stuck with a white, male coach. No wonder I had such a hard time with my speech. He thought I had speaking talent but was not using it. I was just plain scared of him.

I felt intimidated by the coach; he was so sure of himself. He was demanding and critical of my speech. I was not able to realize that he was not criticizing me personally when he talked about the speech. My only close contact before with men had been with Daddy, and so I had never had much of a chance to learn how to relate to them. My problem seemed complex and there was no one to talk to about it.

Somehow I made it through that semester of competing at speech tournaments. I did impromptu speeches, extemporaneous speeches, and oratory. The impromptu speeches were the hardest because I wasn't told the topic until a couple of minutes before I was to speak. Extemporaneous speeches had to be prepared in five minutes. Only oratory was done from a prepared manuscript.

I refused to debate. Debating was the craziest thing I had ever seen and to this day I still don't think a whole lot of it.

The tournaments were nerve-wracking but they provided me with some friendship and fellowship. They also gave me a chance to see some other campuses. Team members were paid a little money for meals, and so I ate very carefully and managed to save some of the money for days at school when I was broke. I never developed the good sense to make a lunch, and so I would go without eating all day and eat all evening at home to make up for the missed meals.

The acceptance of the members and the coach of the forensic team helped me a great deal in my journey. I gained a measure of confidence as I continued to go on the tours. Having to find my way around on campuses such as UCLA and Cal State at Los Angeles helped me too. Those campuses were like small cities and it took a bit of courage and ingenuity for me to get from one place to another.

One thing I did learn about God during those college days was that He uses all of the circumstance of our lives to help us learn His lessons. Depression became an overwhelming force in my life. Somehow I managed to scrape through my first year at college although I barely passed some of my classes. When June came, I didn't have the energy to worry about it; I just wanted to go home to my family.

My first year at college was difficult because I had been so unprepared academically and spiritually for the challenges I had to face. I had also spent too much of my time in my younger years fantasizing about a better life. When college presented me with a chance for a new beginning, I didn't know what to do with the opportunity.

As I think about those Arkansas farm years and my dreams of a better day, I am amused at how long it took me to go from just dreaming to actually making dreams come true. Maybe I had dreamed and dreamed until it became too painful to give up the security of dreams for the reality of college life.

Somehow, I had equated getting away from the farm with success. I had gotten away, but I had not found success. I was embarrassed and bewildered by my failure. My vision of becoming a significant person was dying quickly and I really no longer cared who knew my name. I was beginning to wonder if anyone ever would know it.

God was still a part of my life, but I was not spending much time with Him. I felt cut off from Him. I was lonely; I was tired; I was hurt. I needed help. I tried to get an appointment at the psychotherapy clinic at Long Beach State College, but there was a waiting list. I knew I had to have help and somebody somewhere was going to have to give it to me.

My speech coach became concerned about me and talked with me a little. He did some favors for me and he tried to help me find a job. Because I needed somebody to care about me, his interest and concern helped.

After that first year of college ended, I went back to Arkansas. I was still depressed, but glad to go home for awhile because I felt more secure being back in my old world. That summer, the Watts revolt occurred in Los Angeles and Mama almost made me stay home in the fall. She was afraid to let me return, but after I begged her to let me go, she finally agreed.

That summer at home was spent caring for a little girl and her terminally ill grandfather and cooking in a restaurant. I worked at the man's house form 7:00 a.m. to 1:00 p.m., then went to work as a short-order cook in one of the local hotels from 2:00 to 10:00 p.m.

I made a total of seven dollars a day working on those two jobs. I saved every penny because I wanted to go back to Los Angeles and take care of myself. I wanted to pay my own way back and rent an apartment with a girl friend who had graduated from high school with me. So I saved. I even worked on days when I was sick. I couldn't afford to lose a nickel.

I did it. I bought my own ticket back to Los Angeles, and when my girl friend and I rented our first apartment, I paid my half of the rent from the money I had earned during the summer.

That determination to survive and to make something out of my life kept surfacing enough to keep me going. I was not at all sure I would make it. I just knew I had to keep trying.

This period in my journey with God was probably more doubt-filled than any I had known before. My world had expanded so quickly I didn't know how to handle it. The sustaining force in my life was a very special gift God had given to me—something I didn't even know I had until many years later. The gift was "tenacity." As I see it, tenacity is *the ability to hang on to the rope even when there is no knot at the end of it.*

God in His mercy had given tenacity to me along with my tiny seed of faith. I didn't realize it during those lonely college years, but because He had blessed me with tenacity, I would make it.

The thought of going back to Los Angeles for the second year of college did not fill me with the sense of expectancy the first year had, but I was sure I had to return. I also knew I had to live away from my brother, and without any real skills, I had to find a job. And so I went back filled more with fear than with hope.

I found an apartment the day I returned. It was in a rather run-down part of Los Angeles, but it was all my roommate and I could afford. I never felt comfortable in that place. I was never sure that somebody wasn't going to break into the house when we were there. Sometimes this happened to people in that area. But God protected us and we lived there safely for more than a year.

The first Monday I was back in Los Angeles, I discovered a newspaper ad for a house cleaning job and I called the woman about it. She asked me to come that evening to talk with her. I caught a bus headed in her direction even though I had no idea where I was going or if I could even find her house. I did and she hired me.

The job paid $20 a week and the white family I was working for lived in a little town about fifteen miles from where I lived. I left home at 6:00 a.m. in order to arrive at their house by 8:00 a.m. I worked until 4:30 p.m., took the bus home, and then went to night classes. I had decided to attend at night so that I could have a job.

Sometimes God surprises me with His miracles. There is a part of me that often wonders "Why me, Lord?" He never fails to answer, "Because I love you."

I had been back in Los Angeles for three days, and I had an apartment and a job. God had remembered me and met my needs. My hope began to strengthen and I relaxed a little.

A few weeks after I took the maid job, the family informed me that they were moving to another city. I was bewildered. Where would I find another job? I rode the bus home that night without paying any attention to where I was going. I don't remember how I made it.

My roommate was working as a waitress at a barbecue place. The next morning after I told her about losing my job, she said they needed another waitress at the restaurant where she worked. I went that afternoon and applied for the job. They hired me—I couldn't believe it!

The waitress job had worse hours, but I learned that my days off were the same days I had classes. I was surprised things were continuing to work out for me. My work hours were from 6:00 p.m. to midnight during the week and from 8:00 p.m. to 4:00 a.m. on the weekends. I would work until 4:00 in the morning on Sunday, go home, and sleep until 10:00 a.m. Then I would get up and go to church.

The second semester of my second year of college got off to a better start. I was able to take classes during the day, I met a few people, and my roommate took a class with me. The job at the barbecue restaurant wasn't great, but it helped with the expenses and I didn't plan to be there forever. But I had to take a day at a time. I was still scared.

At the end of the school year, someone told me about a job opening in the credit department of a clothing company. I wasn't sure what my chances were, but I decided I didn't have anything to lose. I applied and they hired me that day. I worked until 5:00 p.m. and then took the bus to the barbecue place. For about ten days I kept both jobs. I don't remember a time before or since then that I have been so tired.

The job at the clothing store was a clerk-typist trainee position. My typing was poor, but I was conscientious and I tried to learn as quickly as possible. The supervisor acted like a slave driver. I think she liked me because she thought I had the makings of a good slave!

It was a nice change because I finally had a job that made use of my brain a little. The work was also giving me some experience so that someday I could do something better. Things were just seeming to settle when my roommate announced that she was getting married.

I guess God will do anything to help us realize that there is no security except in Him. I didn't know anybody else to live with and so I moved in with my half-brother.

After a short stay with him, I found a one-bedroom apartment in Compton. It was in a fairly nice building and was close to campus. The apartment was further from work, but I wasn't looking for heaven on earth; I was just trying to survive. I had very little furniture and the place was not furnished very well. But it was clean, freshly painted, and had a yard. For the first time since starting to live by myself, I wasn't afraid at night.

During a quiet night in my new home, I realized that my life was being moved toward God in a way that surprised me. There was a deeper level of trust in my heart than I had experienced before. It often seems that it is not the big crises of life that teach us trust, but the experiences during slow uneventful days when we are not sure there is any movement at all in our lives. Finally the day comes when we realize that we have been moving along.

The Lord answered my prayers and sent me a roommate, my sister Lena. I was able to find her a job in the credit department with me and she stayed for the summer. We enjoyed going to work together and I liked having her at my little apartment. We had a good summer; I was really sad for a long time after she left.

After Lena left, I realized that I felt tired all of the time. I was always hungry and ate all the food I could find, but I was still losing weight. I thought I would get around to seeing a doctor when I had the money. One evening my brother and his wife came to see me. I must have looked terrible, because my sister-in-law gave me some money and instructed me to go the doctor.

The doctor's office was near my house and appointments weren't needed. He examined me the next day and told me I had to go to the hospital. He thought I had an enlarged thyroid gland which is known as a "goiter."

I was almost in tears because I had to go to work and to school. I didn't have any money for the hospital. I begged the doctor not to send me to the hospital, but he said that I had to go. He won of course.

I spent five days in the hospital. I hadn't realized how exhausted physically, spiritually, and emotionally I was. I slept almost without waking for five days. I would wake up long enough for a meal or a lab test and then I would go back to sleep.

At the end of the five days, I was released to the care of the surgeon. I was to have the goiter removed later, and for six weeks I was to take iodine to help make the thyroid more manageable in surgery.

I felt bewildered and betrayed. I wondered if Jesus had forgotten about me; I didn't understand all that was happening to me. I didn't have the money to pay for all of this. I wanted to go home to Arkansas, but I couldn't. I felt I was alone and I didn't know what to do.

I left the hospital and went home to my little apartment. It was good to be home. I had planted some flowers in the yard and they were blooming. They encouraged me because I could see there was still life and beauty around. Maybe, I thought, the heavy dread and death that I felt in my soul were not the only real things after all. Maybe there was a reason for hope. I really didn't know the answer and there weren't many people around to offer comfort.

I finally managed to get back in the swing of things. The tranquilizers and iodine in my system made me feel better. The thyroid illness had caused me to be nervous and tired all of the time and I had been having trouble sleeping. But now the medication helped me rest better.

I soon realized I couldn't afford my apartment and I had to find another place to live. Some friends had a spare room and they offered it to me. I took it because I was in no position to be "choosy." I just kept wondering why God didn't make things easier. It was an agonizing time.

The Lord seemed to be going to a lot of trouble to teach me that being a Christian didn't mean I would escape hardship. The only promise He had made was, "Lo, I will be with you always."

I finally just gave up. I gave up on college. I gave up on life. I went to the hospital fully expecting to die and never see any of my family or friends again. I didn't care anymore. It was just too hard trying to keep everything tied together with hope. But a very strange thing happened. I found I was at peace for the first time in five years.

No one had come to teach me the theology of "giving up" or any other theology for that matter. The churches I had been attending hadn't done it. No, the Lord was teaching me Himself through circumstances and experiences. I was learning that he could only perfect His strength in me when I became willing to relinquish or "give up" all of my problems and weaknesses to Him. It would be years later before I became aware of the scriptural principles behind the learning experiences I was going through.

My surgeon turned out to be a brilliant black doctor who had graduated from medical school at twenty-two. This was an important experience for me because I had never had a black doctor before. It was especially significant because he was one of the best general surgeons in the country. I had the operation on a Friday morning and greatly surprised myself by waking up in the recovery room sometime later that day. I was surprised because I had been ready to die and was so sure that I would. I felt as if my life had been given back to me.

I went home from the hospital three days after surgery, recovered quickly, and went back to work in a month. I was tired much of the time, but I managed. I went back to school during the second semester. I was going to live! I felt like trying to accept the challenges of life again, and I felt my hope slowly coming back. I was learning that my little seed of faith was going to be nurtured by my gift of tenacity regardless of how many weeds of doubt surrounded it.

Three months after my surgery, I went to work for the surgeon who did my operation. Working for him gave me an opportunity to take more classes because he allowed me to juggle my work hours. What a blessing! I also made twice as much money as I had on any other job.

By the following summer I had rented another apartment because two of my sisters were coming. Lena found a job working for the pediatrician across the hall from my office and Irene worked with me.

God never took His eyes or His hands off us. We often thought that He had, but He kept on being faithful and kept providing for our needs. He opened doors and made ways for us when all the paths seemed to be blocked.

My most vivid memory of how He opened doors concerns the loan I received to complete my college work. I had gone as far as I could at Compton College and needed to transfer. I wanted to move to Pepperdine College because it had a religious emphasis and I wanted to study the Bible under someone who had proper training. The problem with going there was money. I had a National Defense Loan and a speech scholarship, but I still needed more funds.

One day in a rather casual way, I mentioned my need to a man in our office and he volunteered to help me get a loan for the remaining money. What an answer to prayer! The Lord knew how much I wanted to get through college. I had already taken three and a half years to do two years of academic work. I was starting to be afraid I would be in college as long as Mama had been.

My last semester at Compton College had been great. The surgery had provided me with a new perspective on life. I had gone back to school determined to do better. It had been difficult plowing through economics, philosophy, world literature, and international politics courses. But I had been determined, had studied hard, and I did well.

The loans, the scholarship, and the grace of God got me to Pepperdine for the fall quarter of 1967. I felt as if I had embarked upon a new path to find the significance and purpose that I wanted so much for my life.

The thing that surprised me so much then—and still does to this day—is how God calls us to "give up" continually. He will ask us to give up our visions, our families, our friends, and ourselves as well.

This may be why so much of my life has seemed like a cycle of death and resurrection, that process of continually "letting go." The only way to live in any peace seems to be with open hands, because open hands can't hold on to anything.

It has become clear to me that God does not intend for us to cling to anything but Him. This is particularly true in relationships. If we are not careful, our interaction with each other can become calculated manipulations to satisfy our own personal needs.

He calls all of us to let go of each other so that we can be free to care for and experience the beauty of each other. He wants us to let go of our claims to everything in the world so that He can return as "gifts" everything that we really need. After all, the things we have are really gifts. I have struggled long to realize that truth. And I am certain, too, that the struggle is not yet finished, because I am still on a journey with Him.

Chapter 5

Despair and Yet . . .

I felt good about my decision to go to Pepperdine for a major in speech. Speech was one of my strong areas and there seemed to be no reason not to take advantage of that ability.

I must confess that my idealism and my inability to face the political realities of the world made my time at Pepperdine harder than it probably needed to be. But as I picked up class cards and planned for the beginning of class, I was filled with excitement and anticipation. I believed my life was going to be different, and I was right.

Do you know how it feels when your life seems to be caught up in a whirlwind and you are not at all sure the whirlwind won't blow you away? My first year and a half at Pepperdine was kind of like that. It was exciting, but it was also frightening.

When I had still been attending the community college, my sister Lena came to live with me. Now, with my new venture at Pepperdine about to begin, Mama asked Lena and me to let another sister, Irene, come and live with us. I was afraid our agreeing to take care of her was not the right thing to do. But Irene was sick and none of her doctors in Arkansas seemed able to diagnose her case.

Lena and I were rather young to assume the responsibility of raising an emotionally unstable thirteen-year-old. The day she arrived we put her in the hospital for tests. The doctors could find no major physical causes for her discomfort. She had an infection of the thyroid gland, but that was not severe enough to explain her inability to breathe. The doctor referred her to an endocrinologist for treatment of her thyroid. Every Wednesday, which was my day off from work, I had to take her to the hospital for consultation.

After joining us, Irene was sick for about two years with one ailment after another. She spent at least half of her time in the hospital or at the doctor. Finally, we referred her to a psychologist. Thankfully, that referral was the beginning of her journey to wholeness.

But the stress and trauma of our lives together were to go on for a long time. The environment at home was not always pleasant. I felt too great a sense of responsibility for my sisters and I worried about their welfare too much.

My job had its own set of pressures. My work required me to be efficient, and since my boss trusted me, my efficiency was even more essential. School added another dimension to my life. Then there was the journey with God. For more days than I care to remember, I felt like a grasshopper being pulled apart.

It is important that you understand how my life was being affected by the personal responsibilities and struggles that God had given to me. Then you will see why, as I relate the ways He called me to serve Him at school, I can say personal problems do not excuse us from being a servant. This is another of those interesting theological truths that I experienced long before I was able to articulate it.

The great challenge to be a servant was offered to me one Wednesday night about 9:00. The telephone rang and a friend who lived in the dormitory told me to start praying and not to stop. She said that a black child from the local community had been shot on campus by a security guard.

I couldn't believe my ears. I hung up, grabbed my purse, and ran to my car. I prayed as I drove to the campus. I couldn't imagine some boy being shot on our campus. It was such a peaceful place.

The faint question "Why?" started to echo in my soul. Someone told me when I got to the campus that the boy had been dead on arrival at the hospital. Some of us had been getting together to pray during the quarter and so we had established some bonds of concern for each other. We were to realize in the days and weeks to come the importance of that fellowship and how much we really needed each other. But we had too much trauma to face on that Wednesday night to worry about ourselves.

People were everywhere. Policemen. Reporters. Adventure seekers. Friends. Enemies. The world of our campus was turned upside down. The people from the Los Angeles Rumor Control Center were there trying to learn the facts. Answers were being demanded because this was the 1960s and black folks were not tolerating the murder of blacks by whites as they had before.

It appeared that there was no reason for the young boy to be dead. He had been a respected child in the neighborhood who had never caused trouble for anyone. And he hadn't been causing trouble that night.

He and some of his friends had come onto the campus like they always did to play basketball in our gymnasium. But because it was Wednesday night, the time for midweek worship, the gymnasium was closed. The boys were walking around outside, waiting for the gymnasium to reopen, when the security guard decided to make them leave the campus. He confronted them and supposedly asked them to leave. Larry, the child who later was shot, tried to reason with him. He asked the security guard, "Don't you remember me?"

The guard should have remembered him since Larry's mother had asked him before to see if it would be all right for the kids to play in the gymnasium.

That terrible night the guard answered with his shotgun instead of his mouth. He shot Larry in the chest.

Fear. That is why Larry died that night. The security guard had worked on the campus for years. He was there before the community had become more heavily populated with blacks as the whites fled to the suburbs. He was there before the revolt in Watts. He was there when people respected a uniform. It had been a mistake to leave him there as the only security guard for so many years.

He couldn't understand his world anymore. Black people no longer thought white folks were grand just because they were white. You had to do something to earn black respect. Nobody ever told the guard what was going on. He was just told to protect and serve. Sadly, he didn't know that he was to protect and serve black people too.

I strongly believe the security guard never intended to kill that child, and I know he was sorry for it afterwards. He was as much the victim as the person he killed. He had been afraid, and so were we.

The "we" was the Black Student's Alliance (BSA), a group made up of a large cross section of the blacks on campus. Blacks who were not members were fairly unpopular, and so people joined for all kinds of reasons. But BSA membership was not necessary for anyone who wanted to help fight for justice in the case. Loyalty was the only thing we wanted.

One thing needs to be remembered about blacks and the mood of the 1960s: We were afraid. Although we were young, we felt we had to *do* something. Our thinking then was, when you have been unfairly treated and you realize you have no one to turn to, what do you do? We knew the BSA couldn't be choosy about who was in the group. We needed all the help we could get.

Now that the 1970s are here, many of us can now stand for our democratic rights; but in the sixties that was not possible. Then we were tired in so many ways. Tired of injustice and abuse. Tired of young blacks being killed and nobody stopping to mourn their deaths. Tired of their killers going free as it they had done nothing—as in this security guard's case where he was fined and placed on probation.

What do you do when you are scared, young, and tired, but you know you have to take a stand? There were some students in our group who were ready to die for the "cause." It was the age of "causes," and on our own campus a person's life had been taken. I thought that if this was not a worthy "cause," surely there would never be one.

Of course, there were some people in the BSA who were not sure they were ready to die for the "cause." I was one of them. We realized something very evil was happening and we were opposed to evil. We wondered what the Christian faith had to do with this whole struggle anyway. What did God want of us? Our agenda as Christians included more than militancy. We were willing to be militant, but not just for the sake of militancy. This was not an easy issue to resolve.

Caught in the middle of this dilemma, I thought I would ask the people at my church what I should do. At the time we were having strategy meetings in the BSA and some of our plans were dangerous. Somebody was going to get hurt. I was afraid and confused! Surely God didn't want me to practice violence and destruction. And yet, as a Christian, what was my response to be to the overpowering evil of the system? I took my questions to the elders of my church.

It didn't take long for me to realize that, even though I had gone to the right place, the elders had no answers either—only fears. I found that they thought much like some of the administrators at the college. These elders, even though they were black and oppressed, supported the system and were hoping some day to get their piece of the "American Dream Pie." They didn't realize that there was no part of the "American Dream Pie" for them. Black folks and poor folks were never supposed to have any of the pie in the first place. The only way the black and the poor could make life better for themselves was through unity.

I prayed a lot during those days, but I never cried one tear. If I had started, I would have cried myself to death. I knew there was too much pain dammed up behind my wall of tears to ever risk letting it break free.

I had a friend who went through this questioning period with me. She didn't know what to do and was scared too. We both believed in God and we knew He wanted us to hear and obey His Word. But how could we? We kept searching for His leading, but we had to keep walking in what we already knew.

Finally, my friend and I decided we needed to go and see Larry's mother. She had been more of a loser in this situation than any of the rest of us; she had lost her youngest son.

The little green house on the corner where Larry had lived his short sixteen years looked as if it knew all about sorrow. As we entered the house I felt as if the very walls and the floor under our feet were crying out for justice to be done once—just once after a black had died at the hands of a white. I agreed!

Family and friends were there and they were all very gracious to us. The BSA had collected money and had bought food for them. Someone thanked us again for the food even though it had been brought a couple of days before our visit. Larry's mother was in bed. The situation had so disturbed her that she had been given a sedative.

Someone finally told us to go into her room and say hello. She spoke with us, but she had a dazed expression on her face. If she had not been a strong woman, she would not have lived as long as she had. She had a kind of courageous spirit that one could sense just after being with her for a few moments. We left feeling that she would make it, but we wondered if we could.

In the months following Larry's tragic death, many of us spent a lot of time at his mother's house. She loved us as if we were her own children. She cared about the future of each of us and she knew we would make a difference in the world. We often tried to tell her the difference she was making in us by being a part of our world.

It was easy to see that this woman was living her life in close fellowship with God. Although living in the midst of unending despair, she still had peace and courage. She had a kind of serenity that seems to come to those who have suffered and wept, but who have never failed to believe that joy would come in the morning. She was a tremendous lady. I thank God for her.

Larry's funeral was held about a week after his death. People came from everywhere and the church was filled with not only his teachers and friends, but with people who attend funerals only because they have nothing else to do.

The memory of the funeral is forever burned in my mind by a single incident that occurred there. As is the custom in black funerals, the casket was opened for everybody to see Larry's body for the last time. When this was done, his mother screamed out his name and the sound pierced my heart like an arrow. It seemed as if two hundred years of grief were released in that scream. It seemed as if all the years that she and mothers like her had spent scrubbing other people's floors and being dehumanized were expressed in that scream. All of my own disillusionment with a system that doesn't work for poor folks or blacks, and the realization that it never was designed to work for them, were expressed in her scream. I heard the memory of discrimination and the loneliness of racism. All of these lived together at that moment in the tear-stained bosom of this strong, beautiful black mother.

The tremendous thing about her was that she always told us to be forgiving. But how could we when we felt her anguish and ours too?

I honestly found myself wanting to kill somebody that day, just anybody who was white. I finally understood what black rage was all about and why the brothers in the BSA were so hard to reason with. They knew there was no hope for justice or equality in this land unless somebody made it easier to give justice than injustice. It was no wonder that during the week after Larry's death I felt as if I were in a war zone when I was on campus. I was.

Sometime that day, the funeral was over and we made the trip back to campus—a trip that seemed awfully long even though it was less than five miles. When we got back, the reporters were still there. I climbed into my beat-up little Ford Falcon and drove the twelve miles to my home in Compton.

When I arrived, my sisters were very concerned about what had happened at the funeral and how the day had gone. They too had been very disturbed by Larry's death. They also had been disturbed by the response of the church elders to me. They were angry as I was. I was also deeply wounded. Driving back from campus that day, I had wondered deep in my soul where a person like me might find a "home."

As I watched the news reports each evening of what was going in at our campus, I wondered what campus they were talking about. During those days, I questioned if the news media would know the truth if they saw it chasing them?

As I said earlier, many of my college's administrators made an effort to go on with business as usual. There were, however, at least three administrators who did not try to find the easiest way out the situation. As a result, they went through a "hell" that could never be described on these pages.

These three people stand out in my mind because even though they were administrators, they were different. They were committed to truth—or anything else except maintenance of the status quo —during the 1960s. There were many folks who called themselves liberals, but they were not committed to truth. If they had been really committed, they would have realized they weren't really liberals. Evidence of this fact is that many of them today are the very conservative protectors of the establishment.

At any rate, the three people I have mentioned took some giant steps of faith and did the only thing a courageous white person should do: They went to their white sisters and brothers and tried to help them see their need for repentance. For their efforts they received what black folk have been getting for two hundred years: rejection and humiliation.

Their willingness to take a stand did win them the respect of a good portion of the blacks in the student body. It won them my love and respect for the rest of my life. During those troubling days as they pondered the question of what is reasonable service in the kingdom of God, they found the answer to be the laying down of their lives for their brothers and sisters. It saddens me that their establishment sisters and brothers did not recognize the gift God was sending them through these three people.

Black people have learned to take advantage of all opportunities, and there were some who were wise enough to use this tragedy to try and make a step forward. I never did know if all of our efforts were aimed at furthering the cause of justice and equality or just attempting to make some people feel a little better about themselves. But I do believe there were those among us who wanted to see justice triumph just once in our lifetime.

We met every night and planned our strategy to seek protection against injustice. Later we presented some "demands" to the administration. We thought somebody had to pay. Blood had been shed, and a life had been lost. It all had to count for something. We wanted those in the administration to save a little of their integrity and respond to us in a humane way.

We believed the "demands" were reasonable. Among them were requests for the college to pay for Larry's funeral expenses and to set up a memorial scholarship fund for his sister and brother.

Our administrators listened attentively as our demands were presented. They listened so well we almost believed they had heard our despair and desperation.

Later, when we heard the administration's representative promise his constituency that no demands would be met, we knew they had not heard us at all. We knew we had to work not only on drawing up demands, but in giving these people some ears with which to hear.

The thing I had dreaded all along was finally going to happen. We met to plan our first march. I was afraid.

Part of my fear and frustration about marching had to do with the possibility of going to jail. If I did, how would I get the bail money? I felt responsible for my sisters and I did not want to die on them, for I knew that I could be killed. I knew it was possible because I realized that a political system will do anything to protect its existence, and we were dealing with a political system.

I thought about all of this during several sleepless nights. I had told Jesus that I would follow Him. He somehow seemed to be mixed up in all of this, and although I couldn't swear to it, I thought He had called me into it. I talked to my sisters and found out that they were scared too. They thought I had better be careful. I was afraid to tell Mama because I knew she would tell me not to do it. The church people, with the exception of one person, had told me to stay home until the trouble was over. I had nowhere to go but to the One from Galilee, and since He was in the march, it was off to the march for me.

I finally realized what Dr. Martin Luther King had meant when he said, "Until you find something to die for, you don't have anything to live for!" I knew deep in my soul that if I had to die, it would be because I was trying to follow Jesus. I was ready to march and be shot if He would be there with me. And He was there.

Of course I knew that death might turn out to be a lot easier than living. I knew if I lived I might lose my scholarship, I might be kicked out of school, or I might go to jail. Finally, I was ready to face the consequences of marching and I went.

It was on that day I decided that if I were to die, it would be for Jesus and not for civil rights. Civil rights is a noble cause, but not a strong enough call to compel me to lay down my life. Only Jesus could call me to that kind of sacrifice. It was during this time that Jesus became Lord to me.

My outlook on social causes started to develop during those days. I decided I would become involved as He called me to be involved, but the involvement would not be based on some humanistic myth about saving the world. Saving the world is God's job. My job is to go when He calls me and to do what He tells me to do. He called me in the sixties and I went in His name. He met me in the middle of my involvement and He cared for me.

The morning of the march we met in the Academic Life Building, and after choosing partners, we started climbing the stairs shouting that "the administration had lied." We went through every hall in the building and then out across a lawn which was so serene that the sound of our yells shocked me. We then marched to the administration building, which had been locked by the time we arrived. We were forced to stand on the sidewalk and yell our protests.

After about an hour, we dispersed and our spokesmen called a news conference. During the conference we accused the administrators of talking out of both sides of their mouths. They had no answer. What answer is there for deceit? The news conference lasted too long. We were all too distraught to make any sense out of what was going on. The administration finally came up with a plan for meeting with us later. I think our spokesman agreed simply because he was too tired to fight any more that day.

I don't know where the other marchers went, but my friend and I went to the beach. We had to find a place with fewer distractions than the campus.

It was through those many lonely hours spent walking up and down the beach, listening to the waves, and reflecting upon what was happening to us that I realized there was nothing in the "American Dream Pie" for me.

I didn't realize then that there would be many more opportunities later to struggle with this problem, but what had been my basic adolescent commitment to the system was gone forever. I thank God this happened while I still had a good part of my life ahead of me.

During those days I also came to realize that people are more important than institutions. I learned that honesty and courage are more important than expediency, and that there is only room for one God in one's life.

Without their knowing it, my sisters and brothers in the Pepperdine administration did me a very big favor. Their stance during this campus tragedy greatly contributed to my "new way of seeing." I thank them for it.

When the news media completed their coverage of the events, most of the public was aware of what was happening on our campus. Most of the black people in the area knew that the administration was searching for the easy way out. But we stayed with our demands until most of them were met.

It is extremely difficult to assess this period of our history. Who knows what was won or lost? Perhaps the point never was *winning*, but rather the point was *dignity*. How much injustice and dehumanization could a people take before they retaliated—mostly in an attempt to gain some dignity?

Perhaps the struggle on our campus was to call forth the ones who were serious about serving the Master. Following Jesus is not some nice little social event; it is a journey filled with struggle. If we want to follow Him, we have to be ready to be bruised. After all, He was *wounded*. So why should we who come after Him hope to live without being bruised?

Another thing several of us learned from the protest on our campus was that our attitude toward the situation could reflect life or death. We chose life. Although despair was around us all of the time, we had more than that.

I realized how much more than despair I had every time I went to see Larry's mother. The strength of this black woman was a beautiful thing to see. She had survived the faithlessness of her husband, the years of scrubbing floors in white people's houses, the murder of her son, an emotional breakdown, and the amputation of her leg. And yet she could talk about the mercy of God and make you believe her. She had a view of life that needed to be considered by all of us. She continued to have hope until she went home in 1973 to the God she had loved and served for most of her life.

Larry's mother had known all about despair, but she had also known there was more. As a young black woman, I received no greater blessing than meeting and knowing this woman. She was a special lady.

Chapter 6

Becoming Reconciled to Oneness

Reconciling myself to the idea of all believers being one has not been an easy thing to do. I must confess that I have had the most difficulty accepting this notion in regard to race. But if I believe scripture, which I do, then I have no choice but to accept it.

It is rather clear to me that all who have responded to the call of Jesus Christ are indeed one. As I think about some of the people who have responded, I find some who appear to be very unlikely believers. But that does not matter; the way I feel about them does nothing to change the fact that they are my sisters and brothers.

The fact that these "unlikelies" are in the family means I have to love and accept them. Sometimes this truth causes me great anguish because I would prefer to choose whom to love. Yes, there are some people who I would like to leave out, but God will not have that in His kingdom. He has said, "There is neither Jew nor Greek, there is neither bond nor free, there is neither male nor female: for ye are all one in Christ Jesus" (Gal 3:28).

Racial reconciliation is not easy and I am not sure it ever will be easy for me or anybody. But just as we have no choice about whom we will love, we also have no choice about being reconciled racially. To refuse the healing and reconciliation God offers is to shut ourselves off from a more abundant life.

I realized one day that racial reconciliation had something to do with wholeness and that it also meant I would have to face my own prejudice. Therefore, I launched out upon a search for reconciliation, one that started during my first year at Pepperdine. I wanted to feel better about myself and my world, and I wanted some answers to my questions.

Perhaps the courage I found to continue my quest for truth was just another part of God's unrelenting efforts to keep on making me into a new creature. First He gave me the desire to be at peace with myself and my world. Then He began to fulfill that desire as He provided all kinds of circumstances and experiences to help me on my journey. God is truly amazing.

It is important to remember that prior to my college experiences at Compton College I had never had good interactions with white people. All my experiences in Arkansas had been negative.

My memories of the white farm owners for whom my daddy was the sharecropper were negative and made me feel hostile. These farmers all had been racists and red-necks in the truest sense of the word. I hated them because of the things they had done to my daddy. Then there had been the white folks who came to tell Mama and Daddy their bills were past due.

As I ponder the idea of reconciliation, I realize it means loving many of the white folks I have known who have behaved as if the blacks around them were slaves.

In the South we had all of those "colored" signs. A black person couldn't go to the bathroom, get a drink of water, or buy a coke, hamburger, or ice cream cone without going to the place marked "colored." We always had to go around back. I hated those places.

I still feel the anger I felt as a child whenever we had to stand at a back window and wait for service. We never were served until all of the white people had been served. Finally, I acquired enough anger and dignity to refuse to go to those windows.

When I was younger, I liked ice cream cones—and I still do. It may be that those earlier experiences of having to stand in humiliation at side windows just because I was black account for my present excitement about going to buy ice cream cones. I deeply appreciate no longer having to go to a side window marked "colored."

As a young person, the stories about the marches and how the marchers were taken to jail were very hard for me to understand. The most puzzling incident to me was the lynching of Emmett Till. He was accused of whistling at a white woman. I used to worry about something like that happening to my brother.

The news stories about the civil rights movement were sad and I was deeply troubled by them. I worried about Dr. King and used to pray for him.

Perhaps the thing that hurt me even deeper than Emmett Till's murder was the killing of those children in the church at Birmingham, Alabama. I was horrified. I wondered if something like that could happen to my sisters, brother, and me. I couldn't understand why anybody would want to kill children and I shed many tears over their deaths.

I became suspicious of white people and decided they were bad and couldn't be trusted. I had no frame of reference concerning whites—except what I have mentioned. How was I to know there were decent white folks in the world? I was only a child, and none of the white folks I knew showed much decency.

The impressions made upon me in my youth were extremely vivid, such as how it felt to sit in a segregated waiting room at the doctor's office. The silly thing about segregated waiting rooms was that all of us, black and white, ended up being examined in the same examination rooms. The nurses were not very nice to us either. I began to feel there must be something bad about folks like us. The struggle to overcome those early impressions is not over.

About the same time I became angry enough to stop buying ice cream at back windows, I also stopped sitting in segregated waiting rooms. My family would go in and sit down, but I would stand up or stay outside. They would come and get me when it was my turn to see the doctor. My family began to worry that I would get into trouble when I was older.

Since I attended an all black high school, I had no good opportunities to meet white people in any kind of wholesome setting. There was always a distance between any white person I came into contact with and me. It was the type of distance that exists between one who acts superior and one who acts inferior. It was the only way I knew to relate to white folks.

For instance, one summer I cleaned house for a white couple. They were young and fairly nice to me, but I was very ill-at-ease around them. I baby sat for them also and I really liked their little girl. I would be fine as long as they were not home, but as soon as they returned, I always started to wish I could leave. It was such a terrible feeling. I don't suppose, though, that a feeling of inferiority has ever made anyone feel good.

When I left Arkansas and started school in California, I had a lot of adjusting to do. I had to learn how to act around the white professors, counselors, and students who were in my classes. It was to be a long and difficult learning experience. I thank God that

He has helped me to see that being black does not mean I have no tendencies toward racism and outright prejudice; I know I do. However, I know where to find help—the same place I go for forgiveness when I have abused a brother or sister by some other act.

My speech coach at college was a nice person. Racism really made him sick. I remember saying once that I thought the admission policies of the nursing school at Compton College were racist. My speech coach heard this and he later asked me if he could talk to the president of the college about the way I felt. I said "O.K." but I was afraid I would get into trouble.

I felt the admissions policies were racist because of my personal experience of not being accepted by the nursing school. The college catalog clearly stated what the admission requirements were and I had met all of those requirements. I had done well on my entrance exams and my high school grades were good. No one from the nursing school had ever talked with me, and so I didn't know why I hadn't been accepted.

The day after my speech coach talked to the president, I received a call from his office. Can you begin to imagine how scared I was? The president of my college wanted to talk with me! I went to the appointment the next day with my knees shaking.

The president seemed nice enough at the time. I later realized that he was patronizing me and I came to learn how dehumanizing that can be. He was simply a typical white establishment person. He assured me the nursing school was not racist in its admission policies. According to him, the fact that the nursing school had a low percentage of black students (even though overall the college was about equally black and white) had nothing to do with racism. I listened. Finally, I told him that I didn't understand why someone had not explained to me why I hadn't been accepted. He didn't understand it either. He assured me they had a keen interest in having black students.

For some reason I didn't believe him. I didn't think the school really cared about having black students in nursing. However, the next year the director of nursing called me into her office and offered me admission into the program. This was quite strange since I hadn't reapplied or taken any more tests. The invitation surely was not based on the excellence of my first year's work either because it had been a rather hard year and my grades weren't great. It seemed to me that their true admission policy existed some place other than in the catalog!

If you are wondering why I keep talking about my feelings on race, it is because so much of our behavior is determined by how we *feel*. If most of us would act upon what we *know*, we could at least rid the church of racism. As an example, take note of this scripture: "There is one body, and one Spirit, even as ye are called in one hope of your calling; one Lord, one faith, one baptism, one God and Father of all, who is above all, and through all, and in you all" (Eph 4:4-6).

Most of us will believe these verses simply because we believe that scripture is inspired by God. But our feelings make us act as if we disbelieve it. You know what I mean, don't you?

After my years at Compton College, I went to Pepperdine. One summer I met a girl from Pepperdine named Jackie whose uncle was the founder of the college. She was a sweet person who made you feel as if you had known her for a long time.

Jackie was a member of a house church fellowship and a race relations group called Operation Brotherhood. The brotherhood group was composed of staff, faculty, and students from Pepperdine as well as others from the city. Several blacks and about an equal number of whites participated in the group—its purpose being to try to create some honest dialogue between blacks and whites within the group.

We met often and talked a lot. I'm not sure anyone could measure the group's success in any tangible way, but it certainly was important to me. I had never heard blacks and whites talk about the racial situation in this manner before. In this group, I met Dr. Jennings Davis, the Dean of Students at Pepperdine. I also became acquainted with a black girl named Cookye and a black man named Raymond Hamlet. All were to become important persons on my journey of life.

Raymond was one of the angriest black people I have ever met. He was also brilliant. He worked for the gas company and did an excellent job. Raymond couldn't stand white people because he had been hurt so deeply by racism. But he was a Christian and he knew he should try to be reconciled—at least to white Christians.

But how could he be when all he saw was racism and patronizing liberalism? Raymond was very outspoken and articulate, and he impressed upon me the need to be honest always regardless of what you had to say.

Since being with Raymond, I have discovered these words in Galations 5:1: "Stand fast therefore in the liberty wherewith Christ hath made us free, and be not entangled again with the yoke of bondage."

There are so many times I wish that Raymond would have allowed God to set him free. If only he could have accepted the truth that only God can truly set us free. Raymond wanted his white brothers and sisters to make everything better for him. Unfortunately, they were too wounded to provide the healing he sought.

Two years after I met Raymond, he died from cancer. During the very short three months of his illness, I spent a lot of time with him. We often talked about God and heaven. We read the Bible and several books about life after death and he seemed more at peace than ever before. He wasn't eager to die; nobody ever is—especially a person who is only twenty-eight years old and has a wife and two small children. Somehow, I believe Raymond found God's love more through losing his battle with cancer than he could have ever found it in his losing battle with racism. Perhaps he will confirm that when we talk again in the new kingdom.

Sadly, my friend Jackie—who I felt I knew so well so soon—also left my life after I had known her only eight months. She was killed in a car accident. We had talked about Jesus a lot. She just didn't realize she would be leaving so soon to go and be with Him. Neither did I. Her death hurt and shocked me. She had been the first white person who ever invited me to spend a night in her home. She had been used by God in a mighty way to help me see the humanity of white people.

Jackie was the one who had led me to the house church fellowship. I met Karen and Nathan Lane during my first visit to the worship service. They were a young couple who had graduated from Pepperdine and were in charge of the house church. All kinds of people went there—those who had "dropped out" for various reasons, students from Pepperdine, and some who lived nearby in the community. There were few blacks in the church.

The house church was frightening because it was so different. I had never seen women enter into the worship so freely. Although I was not used to the openness expressed there, I sure did crave and appreciate it. I kept going back week after week, and finally, I was attending house church on both Saturday night and Sunday morning.

The House church, my new relationships with white people who were trying to follow Jesus, and my relationships with Raymond and Cookye had a great influence on the way I related to the murder of the young boy Larry. It was during that painful time in my life that some puzzle pieces fell into place for me. Jennings Davis helped me find several pieces, as did two women who worked at Pepperdine, Lucille Todd and Ann King.

Every young black person who seeks racial healing would benefit from knowing folks like them. They are people who have been willing to ask, "What does it mean to follow Him?" They have taken seriously the scripture which says, "Bear ye one another's burdens, and so fulfill the law of Christ" (Gal 6:2). They were people not looking for easy answers and because they sought truth, they followed it when they found it.

Each of them has experienced great disappointment in life, and it has made them sensitive to the burden of blackness. Thank God they are not liberals. As I see it, a liberal is someone who *does not* hold black or poor people accountable because he is not sure they have what it takes to make it. Actually, most liberals seem to me to be rather patronizing.

These friends of mine believed, unlike most liberals, that black folks were equal and could make it in the world if given half a chance. They held me accountable as a *person* and didn't believe my blackness should be an excuse for living beneath my gifts and talents. They demanded personhood from me. They were willing to give me the love and affirmation that made personhood possible. It was their belief in me and their acceptance of me that helped me to realize how important their friendships were. They helped me realize in a deeper way than ever before that people who believe in God have to deal with life differently from those who don't. This is especially true in regard to race relations. They helped me to see that white people suffer too. They helped me to see that all white people are not just interested in maintaining the status quo, and some really do want to know truth.

I guess this awareness became clearer during the campus murder incident because it was then that I struggled so intentionally with what it meant to be both black and Christian in America. I had to come to terms with that issue; I would have never done it without the love of both my white and black brothers and sisters.

Perhaps the greatest conflict came from trying so hard to be sure I wasn't an "oreo." An "oreo" is a black person who is black on the outside and white on the inside. It is not a very good thing to be.

During the 1960s some white Christians thought a black person could not possibly be a Christian if he or she participated in marches and protests. Many of us parted company over this issue. I came to believe that it was impossible to be a Christian and *not* be in the marches. These two perspectives were obviously pretty extreme. But during those days, *extremes* were about the only way blacks knew how to respond.

Some of my friends in the Black Students' Alliance were not sure how they felt about blacks who were Christians. They weren't quite sure we could be trusted. I was not as vocal to them about my faith, but it was never a secret. They were afraid that I might report to "the man." I wish they had known how unlikely that was. I never would have sold out my black sisters or brothers to anyone in the white establishment.

Several times I had to say to Jennings, Lucille, or Ann, "Don't ask me about that because I can't tell you." They honored that request because they respected me and my judgment. They knew my credibility with the BSA was at stake, and they loved me enough to be sensitive to the struggle I was a part of.

Somewhere along the way I came to terms with a very important truth: Jesus calls us to a new order. He requires us to live in a new dimension. I learned I can be who I am because He really has reconciled me not only to Himself, but also to myself and to my world. He says clearly in His Word: "Therefore if any man be in Christ, he is a new creature: old things are passed away; behold, all things are become new. And all things are of God, who both reconciled us to himself by Jesus Christ, and hath given to us the ministry of reconciliation" (2 Cor 5:17, 18). Reconciliation means to restore a broken friendship. I think we all have a bit of restoring to do.

I kept going to see my white friends. I had decided something about this matter of friends while on one of my long walks down by the seashore. I decided that if I was going to be a participant in protest marches, if I was going to chance being sent to jail or being killed for my freedom, then I was going to be truly free. Nobody was going to tell me who my friends should be. That was a tough decision and it wasn't made lightly or easily. But it was the right decision. God had also called me to be willing to lay down my life for my sisters or brothers, and it didn't matter what color they were or how much money they had. Laying down my life was to be my reasonable service.

Being black did not mean that I was exempt from loving all people—yes, even the white folks who were hard to get along with. Now, even though I am still having some difficulty loving a good number of folks, I really shouldn't fuss about it, because love and reconciliation are His will for all of us.

During the trauma of Larry's death, I went for the first time to the home of my white friend Jennings. I knew his wife Vera was pregnant and had been ordered to bed by the doctor. Since the trouble was keeping Jennings on campus a lot, I felt it would be a good idea to go and say hello to his wife. I wanted her to realize that I knew she was having a hard time, too.

I crossed the street to their house and rang the bell. I was scared. What would she think? Here was this strange black kid coming to her house after 10:00 P.M. Someone opened the door for me. I asked to see Mrs. Davis and was shown to the bedroom. I introduced myself and told her why I had come. We talked briefly about the campus situation, and after a few minutes I left.

Four years later, when I was getting ready to leave California, I went by the Davis's to say good-bye. Vera took me in her arms and said, "You are a special person to me. I will never forget that night you came to my house. That really meant a lot to me."

Now do you understand why I believe that to follow God is the most significant thing a person can ever do with his or her life? I would have never gone to see a white woman in the first place if I had been obeying the rules of my culture or the way I felt. I thank God for giving me the grace to follow Him

There were times during my stay at Pepperdine when I had no money to pay the rent, to buy food, or to put gasoline in my car. During one of those times, my friend Lucille gave me a job cleaning her house. I was very grateful. I worked on Saturdays after finishing at my regular job for the doctor. She always paid me well and there were times when she paid me far more than I would have made anywhere else. But it was O.K. because we were sisters and servants to each other. She had some extra money and I had some extra time; we shared them with each other as gifts. How different this work relationship was from any other I had ever had!

As a result of my experience during the struggle after Larry's death at Pepperdine, I became involved in several other endeavors concerning race relations. I became convinced that we have not dealt satisfactorily with the issue of race in this country. Unfortunately, the church, which should have dealt with the issue more straightforwardly than any other institution, has not dealt with it either. Even the more open-minded churches seem to believe the race issue has been settled. I am convinced with all my heart that it is not.

As long as there are liberals who refuse to deal with their personal prejudices, we will have a problem. As long as there is institutional racism, we will have a problem. I think some Christians use their spirituality as a cop-out on racial matters. They pretend they have no prejudice and they probably believe it. This is possible because they are so busy saying "Praise the Lord" that they don't hear Him asking them to be reconciled to their brothers and sisters who are racially different.

Praising the Lord is great. But I think we are at a time and place where the church must deal more directly with racism—especially the racism within its own body. I tire quickly of people who claim to represent the God of the universe and His Son, but all they do is sit around and do nothing. We are told to go everywhere telling people the Good news. Well, part of the Good news is that we can be reconciled to our brothers and sisters. An even more important truth is that we can be reconciled to God and ourselves. We really can become one.

I realize that it is not always easy to know how to be a reconciler. Being a reconciler is also tiring and lonely. It is sometimes very painful. But believers have been called to do it. And if we obey, we no longer get to decide what will happen. But the choice to obey or not is always ours. It may take awhile before we realize that we can choose to obey only because we love Him and want to be obedient to Him and His call.

There are some things I think those of us who claim belief in Jesus should be doing. We need to start by accepting our forgiveness. We need desperately to get beyond that slave/slavemaster mentality we have all inherited. White people have to forgive themselves and their ancestors for their heritage, and blacks need to do the same. We *are* forgiven and it is time we started acting like it. We also need to work hard on accepting one another racially. Of course, the problem with this is that it demands self-acceptance first. I always wondered why Jesus said "love your neighbor as yourself." It is only through grace that we can accept ourselves, and that same grace will help us accept each other.

The acceptance has to go far beyond thinking that somebody is a nice person. It has to be the kind of acceptance that says "I will live in the house with you; whatever I have is yours; I will lay down my life for you." Acceptance is not some nice little social comment; it is a "gut-level" response. We are called at times to make this kind of real response to people who may be hard to love and accept. The only way to arrive at this level with some people is through prayer. But we are called to accept each other, and until we do, we will always be less than we were meant to be.

We need to do some self-examination and to enter into some honest dialogue with one another. This dialogue can be done through seminars, discussion groups, Bible studies, lectures, or other means. Black people need to be involved in this process just as much as white people. We all need to gain a better understanding of our history. White people need to understand what black rage is all about and so do blacks.

We need to talk about our anger regarding race and learn some creative ways to deal with it. One of the best things to happen in my life in the last two years has been my own increasing awareness of my rage. I am angry, and I expect I will be for a long time. There is plenty in this world to be angry about. But I am learning that anger that results in ulcers or strokes accomplishes nothing.

God has called me to deal with my anger creatively. It must be used to help bring healing to others as well as to myself. Even now I see Him bringing healing into my life regarding this matter. My prayer is that believers everywhere will face their anger head-on, deal with it honestly, and then harness it for good results.

The final thing we all need to do is to reaffirm that Jesus Christ is Lord. He is our common ground. How sick I am of both white and black Christians saying that they don't have anything in common! We have Him in common. What else do we need?

I think what we really are saying much of the time is that we don't want to get together. We are afraid of oneness. We like our separation. This separation makes us feel secure because we have always had it. But Jesus calls us to give up our security—both physically and emotionally—and so the separation has to go.

Recently, a commission studying the probability of street violence in America predicted that in the future we will have violence again like that of the 1960s. The commission said that the lack of jobs, crowding in the cities, and racism would be part of the cause. its recommendation was that we get ready to deal with this violence in a militaristic way. So our cities are stocking up with more riot weapons and are preparing to kill rioters.

What else clan you expect from Caesar? But I do expect more, much more, from the church of my Lord. I expect us to find some creative ways to face some of these problems. I personally am seeking every day to deal with racism in my world and in myself so that healing can come to both. I challenge you to join with me in this ministry. God bless you.

Chapter 7

Loneliness

During my college years, I developed a deep desire to share the knowledge and hope I had been given with other black people. I thought that having this desire and being black were enough. Much to my surprise, they were not.

After graduating from Pepperdine University, I never had any intentions of moving to Macon, Georgia. I was planning to live in Atlanta, but after three months of fruitless job hunting in Atlanta, a job at the Bibb County Mental Health Center in Macon sounded more attractive. Perhaps if I had known how painful the work and living experiences in Macon would be, I might not have been so enthusiastic. I am thankful for the slow revelation of God's plan.

The grass-roots black people, who were seventy percent of our patients at the clinic, did not trust me. They could not believe I was for real. They wanted to know why a black person who had managed to escape the South had been foolish enough to return. Whenever I responded to that question with the answer, "I want to serve the people here," they trusted me even less.

I felt alienated from the people whom I had come to serve. I was bewildered and oftentimes frightened. Along with these negative feelings from blacks was another kind of alienation from my white co-workers.

Many of them were very ignorant of what the lives of their black patients were really like. They were racists who were making no effort to change. Everyday I became so angry I felt I would explode into a million pieces. My co-workers were confident of their diagnoses and their treatment plans. They believed they were the healers. I fumed.

My alienation and anger created a depression in my soul that lasted from January 1973 to September 1974. Perhaps the most pain came from realizing that my education and my job in the clinic made me unworthy of trust. I was suspected of being middle class and not being "black" enough to know what it was like to be poor, black, and emotionally unstable. A knife stab in the heart could not have hurt me more than this rejection by the people I wanted to love. Besides, we were a part of one another; our roots were the same. How I longed to have them understand.

After twenty-one months of this hell, I couldn't stand it any longer and decided to leave the clinic. I was losing myself. I would have committed suicide if I had stayed there six more months.

I had always held onto the thread of belief that God had sent me to Macon. But if He had sent me there, then maybe He would help me to leave too. I wasn't sure, but I was at the end of my rope and I just threw myself on His mercy. He proved Himself faithful just as He always had in the past.

Two months after my resignation, I was given a job in Memphis with the city school board as a school social worker. This job offered me a second chance at trying to relate to my black brothers and sisters in a meaningful way. I just wanted to share by blessings and be a servant.

The opportunities to serve were great, and I was so relieved to be out of Macon that it was three months before I had even one criticism of Memphis. I realized for the first time what it must be like to get out of jail. I had been set free! I was free of white professionals who enjoyed their ignorance far too much to seek knowledge; free of my black sisters and brothers who had been hurt too many times by black and white "do-gooders" to believe I was for real; free from the loneliness of living in a world of rejection. I was overwhelmed by my sense of relief.

God was being true to Himself. He was healing me and I was thankful. You can easily see why I never hoped to see Macon, Georgia again. But with God, you're not always able to guess what will happen next in life. I suppose He wanted me to realize that whomever He heals is truly a whole person.

In April, 1975, while thinking of possible summer jobs, I decided to check on an Upward Bound job I had held at Mercer University in Macon during the previous summer. Sure enough it was still available and I was rehired. I was to be the head resident in a women's dormitory for six weeks.

As I left Memphis on a cloudy and humid Friday in June, I was overwhelmed by the peace in my soul. I was on my way back to Macon and was filled with joy and peace! Even more than that,

I was excited about going back. If I had doubted God's ability to work miracles before, I thought I never would again.

During that summer I thought a lot about my future and the kind of work I wanted to do. The school social work position in Memphis was good, but I knew I didn't want to spend the rest of my life doing that kind of work.

I often though about gifts and seriously wondered if I had any. I talked with my friends about spiritual gifts and asked them to point out what they thought mine were. I learned that discovering your gifts takes longer than one summer. However, I did manage to decide which kind of work I thought might be enjoyable and might help me discover my gifts. The choice was student personnel work in a college. I felt this type of job would give me a chance to use my counseling skills and develop my creativity. It would also give me an opportunity to share my faith with many young people searching for the meaning of life.

Since I had not finished my master's degree, I decided that going back to school should be the next step. I filled out an application for Memphis State University and signed up to take the Graduate Record Exam.

A few days after completing my applications, I went to see the Dean of Students at Mercer University. I had not seem him all summer because he had been away four days each week attending school. He happened to be in the day I went by his office. We chatted for a few minutes about our past school terms and the activities of the summer. Then out of nowhere he said, "Why don't you come and work with us next year? We have an Assistant Dean of Women position available." I thought I was dreaming and I felt like the dream could turn into a nightmare at any moment. It was one thing to live in Macon for the summer, but to come back for any longer? Well, I didn't know how I felt about that.

I laughed and said, "You are kidding!" But he wasn't. Finally, I collected myself enough to ask a few questions about the job. After a few more minutes, I left his office after promising to think about the offer. I was flattered, and the lack of a master's degree was not important. I realized about three o'clock the following morning that I had to consider this offer seriously. Too much had already miraculously happened for me to dismiss it as an accident or a coincidence.

After several days of wrestling with my feelings and trying to hear the will of God in this situation, I decided to accept the job.

It took a couple of weeks for the reality to sink in. I had not only decided to take the job, but I had also decided to move back to Macon. But God is faithful. His plan is always perfect and His healing is complete. I was ready to come back to Macon because I felt certain that God was calling me to return. I must confess I wondered what on earth He was so determined for me to do in that town. He was going to great lengths to bring me back there. I was anxious to see His plan unfold.

One concern I had was whether I would find a suitable church when I returned to Macon. My fellowship with God's family in Memphis had been beautiful. I wasn't sure there would be a place in Macon that could provide the friendship and fellowship I had grown to cherish.

One Saturday night after moving back to Macon, I began to pray for guidance from the Lord to help me to choose a place to worship the next day.

The next morning I put on my best dress and gave careful attention to my make-up and my hair. I wanted to be a well-groomed ambassador and to feel confident enough about my appearance not to be distracted as I met people. Sometimes I worry about how I come across to people and forget the importance of being sensitive to the person I am meeting. I didn't want that to be an issue on this day.

I arrived at the church at 10:55 and happily marched into the building humming a song. I was so much at peace and so glad to be alive. As I entered the front door, a little man came up to me. He had his hands clasped behind him and seemed rather embarrassed. I spoke to him and smiled. I was so happy and I was very eager to share my joy.

He said, "Can I help you?"

I was surprised at his question, but assumed he was trying to be polite. I said, "What time does your service start?"

He told me it started at 10:55 A.M. I was relieved to discover I was not late.

I walked over to a table, picked up an order of worship sheet, and waited for the congregation to finish singing. I was humming the song and reading the order of worship when suddenly a group of about ten men came around the corner. I thought they must be ushers, but they came directly to me. I was surprised when a little fat man leading the group spoke to me with obvious anger and hostility in his voice. But the anger in his voice was minute compared to the hatred in his eyes and face.

"I am the chairman of the board and I want to know what your business is here?" he snapped.

I said, "I am Cathy Meeks. I am a Christian, and I have come here to worship." He glared at me as if I were evil personified and he were charged with ridding the world of it. "I have some friends who used to worship here," I said.

"No you don't," he replied.

"Yes, I do." I told him their names, but he pretended he didn't know them. One of my friends had been a deacon. Since my interrogator was chairman of the board, he should have known him.

They all stood there glaring at me. I was starting to feel weak in my knees and I was sensing a deep desire to be some place else. Finally, I said, "What's the problem? Don't you let black people come to this church?"

He said, "No, we don't."

I said, "That's very interesting," and walked out of the building to my car. As I unlocked the door, I felt more deeply hurt than I had ever been before. I had never been thrown out of any place before and certainly not out of a church. I got into my car and locked the doors. As I started the engine, I burst into tears. I felt so alone. There was nowhere to go and there was no one to talk to. I felt betrayed by the One who seemingly had sent me to be sacrificed at this place. I just wanted to worship in His house with His people, and He had sent me to this place. I wondered why? I was confused.

As I drove home that morning three very beautiful and graceful deer came out of the woods and crossed the road. As I stopped to let them pass, God spoke ever so gently to my hear and said, "There is still beauty in My creation." I knew then that He was faithful and would see me through even this rejection. He hadn't forgotten me.

That afternoon, after I had cried for awhile and prayerfully tried to decide what my response to this incident should be, I decided to call the pastor and ask him if his church had a written policy prohibiting blacks from coming into the building. I thought the church might appreciate learning that discrimination had been declared illegal. The pastor was nice to me and was very apologetic. He said the church was in an uproar about the whole matter. "Our church is going to be split and I just don't know what is going to happen," he said. I felt both anger and pity for him.

After a few more apologies, he asked if he could come to my house for a visit. I said this would be all right, but I made it clear that I didn't need his sympathy. All I wanted was the freedom to worship wherever I wished to. I asked him to call me before he came to my house since I worked every day.

The Wednesday after the incident I came home for lunch and found that the pastor had been by and left his card in the door. I thought that he might call later. The next Saturday I cam home after shopping and he had been by again and left his card. I was enraged! To me this was game playing. It really was irrelevant to me whether I saw him or not; after all, it had been his idea.

I called and told him I would be home the rest of the day if he wished to come and see me. He came by later that day, and by the time he left, I felt more pity for him than anger.

I learned he had been the minister of this church for nine years and he really didn't know the people. He had lived in an unreal world and was comfortable and secure in his ignorance. Now he was being disturbed by truth and he was miserable. He told me some people in the church thought I had been sent. I replied that they were right, I had been sent—not by any civil rights group— but by the One who wanted so desperately to speak to them if they would only listen.

He said that the church had never had a problem before. I asked "How many blacks have you had before?" He said, "None." No wonder they had never encountered a problem!

He left my house promising to let me know if they voted to allow blacks to attend. He never communicated with me again after he left my house that day, and I have never felt led to communicate with him. I don't know what they decided. I pray often for them and sincerely hope they will choose to follow God. Of course, that Sunday morning incident means they will never be the same again, and I must confess, I won't be either.

That Sunday when those men stopped me from worshipping in their church, I experienced one type of painful loneliness. But I have found that loneliness comes in all kinds of shapes and sizes. It can catch you off guard sometimes. The other day I took a couple of pies to a kind old man who takes care of my yard. He appears to be old enough to retire, but death will probably be his retirement date because he is poor and black and probably can't afford to retire.

He is always doing extra things for me. For instance, he will carry my small individual trash can to the large can even though he doesn't have to. He will sweep my porch off whenever he cuts the lawn, and he doesn't have to do that either. He takes his job seriously and it is important to him to do his best. He is a refreshing person to have in a world where many people want to escape working at all. I appreciate him very much.

But this dear man, who has every right to dignity, refused to look at people when they talk to him He has talked to white people a whole lifetime without looking at them. Those eyes might betray him. They might reveal how angry he is and how deep is his disgust toward whites. So he looks at the ground.

When I brought him the pies he wouldn't look at me. It hurt me to have only the top of his greasy gray striped cap to talk to. I wanted to scream at him "I am not white! I won't hurt you! I know what it's like to be black. You can trust me. Besides, I am angry too!" But instead of screaming, I spoke quietly. When I finished, he turned and left with the pies.

As I walked up the street to my little house, I realized that tears were streaming down my face. I kept asking myself, "How can a black woman who has gone to one college and now has a job at another college prove to the black man who takes out her trash that she loves him? How can I show that I love him because he is a part of what I am and I am a part of what he is? How can I tell him that we were both made by the same loving Father?" I wanted him to know that we were not inferior or superior to one another.

Sometimes it seems as if some canyons are too wide for bridges. I pray I will have the courage to keep trying to build them anyway.

I know many white people reading this will want me to know that loneliness is not only a condition of one's race. They will want to say, "How about the times when I have waited all week for a letter to remind me that somebody knows I exist? Then on Saturday the mailman came and he didn't even stop at my house. Or how about the time my best friend, who was only twenty-eight, died of cancer? Or the time when I had an idea about the best way to do a job and no one paid any attention to me?"

My answer to all of these questions is simply, "I know." I have had all of these experiences in addition to the others I have already talked about. I still believe the loneliest person in the world is a black person in a white society. He has the potential to be twice as lonely as a white person.

Another example of the loneliness of being black occurred one time when I went to browse at a local bookstore. In the process of looking, I discovered there were hardly any books by black writers. After a few minutes I was in tears. The tears came because I suddenly felt insignificant and disregarded. The bookstore owner probably had not systematically decided not to order books by black authors. It just never occurred to him that there were any other books to be ordered. It was a simple matter of unconscious disregard. In a situation like that, I would have felt better with an open expression of hostility. At least a hostile word or action would have to be directed toward me and would require a little regard. My point is would a white person ever have this same experience?

Perhaps those angry voices of the sixties, who cried out that it was too hard to be black in this culture, had a valid point. Unless we find some strength outside of ourselves, it is too hard.

Chapter 8

"Lord, Thanks for Tami"

God has given me a very special friend who has taught me more about being human than anybody else in my journey to wholeness. Her name is Tami. She is ten years old and I have known her since she was two.

When she was about four years old, Tami's parents would let her spend the night with me and she would always sleep in bed with me. She would snuggle up real close, and no amount of moving her to the other side of the bed could keep her from snuggling. I finally decided to stop bothering her and let her be.

Tami taught me how to play again. So much had happened to me by the time I met her that I had lost most of the child in me. I had lost the freedom to play. Tami is a physically beautiful child, but her outward beauty is nothing compared to the beauty in her little sweet soul. More important is the fact that she loves me. It makes no difference to her that I am twenty-one years older or that my skin is a different color than hers. She loves me.

I will never forget her anger when I moved back to Macon and couldn't find a place to rent. I stayed with Tami and her parents for a few days. One day I came back to their house after apartment hunting for hours and being turned down repeatedly on the basis of race. I was crushed and started to cry as I told them about my defeat. Tami was enraged and was ready "to go and get those people!"

Later she said, "I am sorry that all those people were ugly to you," and I knew she meant it. It seems children are so much more real than we adults are. They don't play games and they are totally accepting.

Tami doesn't care about my faults; she cares about me. She likes to arrange my jewelry box when she comes to visit. It doesn't bother her that I always mess it up after she straightens it out. I am a special human being to her. She loves me and God knows that I love her. Tami knows it too.

God has spared no effort to provide people and experiences that will insure I have a chance to become a whole person. Lucille Todd is one of those He has used to help me, especially with the issue of racial identity.

She used to spend hours talking with me about dreams, struggles, defeats and victories. She loved me just as I was. It didn't matter to her that I didn't know who I was or where I was going. She was on a journey and she knew who she was; my lack of wholeness was not a threat to her.

Lucille was able to struggle with the issue of race at a deeper level than I was accustomed to seeing in a white person. She knew how much we all had been damaged, both black and white folks, and she was willing to address the issue with me. She shared Lillian Smith's book *The Killers of the Dream* with me. This book deals with what racism has done to whites, and it really helped me to have a little less disgust for white folks and their racism. Lucille and other friends even now continue to be vulnerable enough to me so that I can realize that white people don't have it "all together" either. They need healing just like I do.

I have another special white friend who has helped me with that realization too. He used to say quite often, "I am no better off than you are." I never believed him because I thought a person who was not black was automatically better off. When I finally accepted the truth of his statement, we began to have a freer relationship. I began to see that he needed the Lord's healing just as I did. Regrettably, my wounds did not allow me to see that for such a long time.

All of these people have helped me see that Jesus has provided for me to become a more complete human being. All the help I need has been provided. I don't have to spend the remainder of my life wondering if healing is possible. I know it is because I have experienced it. I finally have claimed the truth of these scripture verses for my own life: "Surely he hath borne our griefs, and carried our sorrows: yet we did esteem him stricken, smitten of God, and afflicted. But he was wounded for our transgressions, he was bruised for our iniquities: the chastisement of our peace was upon him; and with his stripes we are healed" (Isa 53:4, 5).

I am also realizing that not only am I healed by His wounds, but at times others are healed by my wounds. I have pointed out several times that our own personal pain is no excuse for not serving. It seems to me that—even though we may have wounds—in the process of giving, we experience healing. Maybe it's just that when we take our minds off of ourselves, we start feeling better.

At any rate, because of Jesus and His love, acceptance, and friendship, much of the damage in my own life has been healed. This healing is very much a process. I know there are areas of my life that still aren't healed, but that's O.K. I have caught a glimpse of "who I am" and I can live with the unhealed parts.

I have learned to be patient toward my unhealed parts and to pay attention to them in a new way. Whenever we are not sure of who we are, we encounter many threats to our security. We can never really settle down and relax. We have to keep our defenses up at all times. Thank God it doesn't have to always be that way.

I know some of my black brothers and sisters will scream that I have not placed enough emphasis upon race. They will wonder if my fear of being an "oreo" is not a well-founded one.

My answer is that I have come to realize an "oreo" is not somebody who is black on the outside and white on the inside, but a person who does not know who she or he is. Back in the 1960s when we were trying to define our black personhood by one general definition instead of individual ones, we made no allowance for people to struggle themselves with who they were. Our only interest was in who we were as a group.

Back then if a black person liked classical music instead of blues, ate roast duck instead of chitterlings, or preferred sunsets to parties, there was no place for him or her because we were afraid of anyone who was different. We had to be afraid because we weren't sure of ourselves.

For my white reader, I want to make an important point here. Black folks tried to buy into "whiteness" one hundred percent for an awfully long time. And so when the civil rights movement began and the black revolution of the 1960s followed, it was extremely liberating to yell with Stokeley Carmichael, "I am black and I am proud."

Any suggestion of "whiteness" in a black person had to go—it was a matter of survival. Nobody suspected of being less than 125 percent black could be tolerated. There was too much fear to allow for an individual search for self-identity.

However, black people in the 1970s need to struggle with this issue of identity in a new way. We are not the same folks who sat at lunch counters in the 1950s and marched down streets of segregated cities in the 1960s.

We are different because the whole world has changed. This new search means we need to ask quietly in our own souls, "Who am I?" "Who am I when I am alone?" "Who am I when I have lost my place of position and my prestige in the culture?" "Who am I when I am tired and unproductive, when everything is going wrong?"

"Who am I?" I asked that question of myself hundreds of times as I drove home in tears from counseling sessions at the clinic in Georgia. My clients were all so much like me. I wondered how sane they were and how insane I might be. If sanity consisted of being different from them, then I was too much like them to be comfortable.

This same process went on in terms of race. As soon as I would decide that something was a characteristic only of being black, it would turn up in a white client. I was shattered every time this happened because I had so few positive images of myself as black, female, Christian, single and professional. And yet they kept being taken away.

During this time, I would lie awake at night and think. Sometimes I would cry, but most of the time I just thought about things. God refused to let me go. If He had, I would not have made it.

The death of my false soul and the rebirth of my real one was no easy process. All of the images began to leave me and I didn't know who I was. I finally was able to admit that to a friend.

On the day I admitted not knowing who I was, I began to be set free. God was then able to show me who I was as a human being, as His servant, as a black person, and as a person in general. He was also able to show me who I was as a woman, as a single person, and as a professional. It was only a small beginning, but it was a beginning and I was grateful.

It is time for black folks to take up the cross and follow Him to personhood and wholeness. It is time to forget about the past and to forget about what is wrong with us. The Man from Galilee has surely borne our griefs and carried our sorrows and by his stripes we are healed.

One question continues to echo in my heart and mind: "Do we want to be healed?" Personhood, or knowing who we are and accepting it, demands that we seek His healing and become willing to let go of our best sicknesses, you know, the ones that make us feel secure and superior to others.

My point is that it is important not to take shortcuts on our journey to personhood or to make cheap substitutions for selfhood.

For example, trying to be spiritual instead of relating honestly to yourself and others will almost kill you. I discovered this truth after many painful relationships and many broken-heart experiences because people didn't recognize me as a human being. Now there is nothing wrong with being spiritual. You should realize by now that I believe in spirituality, but I believe in it as a gift. The gift needs to be cultivated; it cannot be manufactured.

Don't you know how human our Lord Jesus was? He cried and was lonely. He had to because the Scripture says that He was tempted in all the ways that we are. In addition to being God, He was awfully human. Yes, He really does understand what my burdens are like. I haven't always known this truth; it would have made a difference if I had.

As I accept who I am, my racial identity becomes less of an issue. If we had known in the 1960s that our biggest struggle was with "Who am I?" instead of "Who are we?" we would have been much better off. Acceptance of our racial identity diminishes the chances that we will try to be somebody that we are not. Of course, so does realizing who we are, because after we realize and accept that, there is no longer a need to try to be somebody else.

Blacks are called by the same Lord who calls everybody else. Our communities are filled today with people who think they can escape the cross. If you think that, you are mistaken. Any hatred, anger, bitterness and unwillingness to accept yourself, your brothers and sisters—whether they be black or white—cannot remain. You will have to be healed. God demands it. No one will ever see the Father without going through the Son, and Jesus requires wholeness.

I thank God that He has helped me both to see this truth and to have the courage to struggle with it. A tremendous joy will come to your heart and mind when you finally realize that it doesn't matter whether you like sunsets or parties. You are so much more than what you enjoy.

Whether you are black or white, my challenge to you is this: If you have not already started your search for self, then you need to get started. It will be slow and painful, but you will be glad that you started and so will I. Since we are a part of each other, I will benefit from your struggle to grow just as you will benefit from mine. Keep the faith.

Chapter 9

Joy Will Come

A student came up to me in chapel the other day and said, "Guess what I am going to do on Friday?" "You are getting baptized," I answered.

"How did you know?" he groaned. It was easy; he looked better than ever before.

For some time Mike had been dropping by my office to share his journey with me. He had been having a hard time. He had tried to embark upon a journey of self-discovery, but his peers had become a bit threatened by his "differentness" and were not always very kind in expressing their disapproval. He went through a very personal hell, but usually kept quiet about it. He was (and is) a very warm and sensitive young man and not afraid to cry. I am impressed by men who have the courage to cry.

We talked on several occasions and one day I told him that he needed to settle his relationship with Jesus Christ and be baptized. He listened. Then he left and never came back. I prayed for him and waited. I trusted God to take care of him. That day when I saw him in chapel, I just knew.

My work on a college campus continues to teach me much about waiting. You have to be patient with students. There are many areas in their lives that need to be healed. I have learned that the only way to bring about a change in them is to give them the space and time they need for growth. This is not always easy, but it certainly is a necessity.

Recently, I had a very special experience with another one of our students. A sociology professor invited me to serve as one of several guest lecturers for a class on women in society. I was supposed to talk about the black woman. My interest and enthusiasm for this topic caused me to organize my material early so I could be as effective as possible.

The first day I lectured, the students wanted to talk about racism and race relations and we almost got completely off the subject. I was frustrated. There was one student (I'll call him Jack) who in particular was extremely hostile. By the second day, I was ready to tell him to go fly a kite. I did tell him he needed to visit the library and do some research if he were going to talk about black people.

My disappointment was great. I didn't feel I had communicated much at all about the black woman. The hostility of some people had made me angry and I had become defensive. I was angry with myself when I returned to my office after the last class meeting.

Later in the week I was saddened as I reflected upon the reason for some of the students' reactions. I started praying for all of the students who had been ugly and for Jack in particular. I wanted to love him, but how could I? He had hurt my feelings badly and it was going to take a while to forgive him.

One day about a week after the classroom experience, a student —who had needed a quiet place to study and was practically living at my house—came by to pick up some of her belongings. She told me that Jack was taking her to the mall. Almost without thinking, I said, "I am going with you." It was strange for me to say that since I didn't need anything at the mall and I had tons of work to do. But somehow it seemed like a good opportunity to get to know Jack a little better.

Needless to say, Jack was surprised, but cordial, when I came out and got into the car. We talked about all kinds of things while driving to the mall—his summer job, his new car, my work in student personnel. He seemed genuinely interested in me. After about forty minutes of window shopping and talking, we went back to the car and drove home. We said our goodbyes and wished each other a happy summer.

After they left, I put a potato in the oven and was taking a quick nap before dinner when the doorbell rang. I was aggravated, I didn't want to talk to anybody. When I answered the door, there was Jack and his friend with some bags of fried chicken. Jack had thought it would be nice to bring me dinner. I usually don't eat fried foods, but on this occasion it wouldn't have mattered what he brought. We visited while we ate fried chicken, corn-on-the-cob, and cole slaw. It was a great meal.

God had allowed us to have an interesting encounter as our paths crossed. I pray for Jack often and I believe God will give him the wholeness he seems to be seeking. All I can do is wait and see.

I am sure you know all about waiting on God, and you also probably know about the joy that comes when we have the patience to give God a chance to reveal His dreams and visions for us. It is not easy. As a matter of fact I hate to wait. I usually want things to happen quickly, but God takes His time.

In the Bible we see Him taking His time as He dealt with Abram and Sarah. Just think how many years they spent waiting for Isaac to be born. Can you imagine how hard it was for them? They had been promised a son and God had been faithful in keeping many other promises, but they were getting old. They must have wondered if He had forgotten them.

I can understand why Sarah tried to work the situation out herself. That is one of my greater struggles. After all, God has given me skills and wisdom, so why not use them? The problem is that when our gifts are used to run ahead of His perfect plan, we get into all kinds of trouble. Sarah can bear witness to that.

Then I am reminded of Noah. For many years he worked on the ark and preached, but nobody believed him. People probably thought he was crazy and he may have begun to wonder himself. But he waited and preached and God was faithful.

Of course no list of "waiting servants" would be complete without Jesus. As I reflect upon the scripture, "He learned obedience through the things that he suffered," I wonder if having to wait wasn't one of the things He had to suffer? Waiting is usually very painful for me. If He understands all of my suffering, then perhaps it is not fantasy to think that waiting was not easy for Him either.

We must also be aware that waiting does not always mean something grand and good will happen when the waiting is over. Oftentimes we can sense that God has called us to wait. We don't really know why, but we bear the burden of it for however long He decides, and then it leaves. No bells ring. We don't see any tangible results. That's often the way it is in the kingdom.

However, even in those times when there is no apparent reason for the waiting, we learn to be more patient with ourselves, with others, and with God. Sometimes the dreams and visions become clearer and we can see our selfishness. Therefore, no period of waiting is ever insignificant.

I have lived most of my life waiting on the Lord. It has not been easy and it is still by far the most difficult thing for me to do on my journey with God. In fact, this chapter has been very difficult for me to write because I have been forced to admit that God calls us to be people of patience. Once I write this down and admit it to be truth, then I am committed to trying to live by it. Being patient is very hard for me because there are so many unfinished agendas in my life; it is not always easy to move at God's pace.

Perhaps you are a person who has waited thirty years for a loved one to come to Jesus, and you wonder if the person will ever find Him. Maybe you are having to be patient while your young, ambitious husband attempts to make himself salesman of the year. You may be suffering from a terminal illness and finding it difficult to understand why. Your life may be restricted because you are a mother with small children. You may have been given a special vision of some blessing God has in store for you, but he didn't bother to tell you how long you would have to wait for the fulfillment of it. Yes, waiting can cause you to weep, but the good news is that joy does come—not always on the day that you expect it, but it comes.

God has finally been able to teach me that He doesn't make us wait just to show His power and greatness. He makes us wait because He knows what is best and sometimes we can't realize that in our haste to reach a goal.

As a new and very unseasoned college administrator, in my haste to achieve my goals, I experienced a good bit of disappointment. Some of it was a direct result of not spending enough time waiting to see what I was being called to do. Many times it was shattering when I was criticized for some project I was involved in. So much of my ego was involved in my work. I found it difficult to relate to many of the people I worked with. I was afraid of some of the professors. I felt they would view my outlook on life as too simplistic.

Yet God seemed to have called me to the job. I felt certain of that most of the time, but I let my fear of being rejected keep me from being myself, and that made me appear patronizing. God used the anguish of that first year to help me be more willing to say whatever He wanted me to say and to be myself. It surprised me that it took a whole year to learn that.

Having to wait to see some of my deepest and most precious dreams realized has made me more willing to listen to other people and to share their dreams. I learned, for example, that some of the professors who frightened me most shared common dreams with me.

Whenever you feel you are being called to something, but it is difficult to see how it will be realized, let me encourage you to be patient. It has taken fifteen years for the vague dream of wanting to write a book to become a reality for me. God gave me the vision a long time before He gave me the opportunity to write. He has worked out the details and done a fine job of taking care of things.

A few weeks ago I went to a picnic. The tables were overflowing with goodies, such as salads and the cakes and pies I enjoy so much. It seemed as if everybody had brought their best. Thank God I wasn't even tempted to eat the things that would have caused me to gain weight. The victory over eating too much food came after ten years of praying, soul searching, and dieting. Actually, there had been times when I didn't think God could help me and I thought I would be fat all of my life. Then one day He impressed upon my mind the following scripture: "But they that wait upon the Lord shall renew their strength; they shall mount up with wings as eagles; they shall run, and not be weary; and they shall walk, and not faint" (Isa 40:3). What a renewal of my strength and a joy to my soul when I can now refuse to eat cake or to overeat in general.

I love the college students I work with. Most of my relationships with them have been very reinforcing. I don't know all of them personally, but my prayers are with them. When students are difficult and have to be disciplined, I try to pray for them even more. It seems that the troublemakers are always the ones who are hurting the most inside, and some of them are hard to love.

There are days when a student will come to my office looking for encouragement and I don't have any to spare. Other days someone will come looking for a short-cut to wholeness, but I can only share the insight I've been given that wholeness comes from taking up a cross to follow Jesus and waiting for Him to lead.

Sometimes, I receive notes from students who have realized that my life is not always easy and they want to encourage me. Perhaps the highlight of my experiences the first year came when a group of students showed their appreciation for me by taking up a collection and buying me a little cross and a jewelry box. I was humbled and deeply grateful.

Life on a college campus moves fast and is full of excitement. There are lectures, concerts, and many opportunities to meet interesting people. The students provide a lot of the excitement. They are fresh and many are enthusiastic about life. They add a beautiful dimension to my life.

But even in this stimulating environment, there is another side to my life. There are days when the routine and the sameness of every activity bores me. There are days when I am called to bear someone's burden, a burden that feels like it would be too heavy for twenty people. There are days when lectures are cancelled because of snow or illness. There are days when guest speakers don't do a very good job but must be paid anyway.

There are times when I wonder what I am doing in this place and what education is all about. The days of doubt, loneliness and waiting are still a part of my life. Sometimes I don't make it home before the tears start to fall quietly from my eyes. And then there are the days when the pain dries the tears up and there are none.

It is not all glamour and excitement. It is not all joy. It is very ordinary and tiring. It is just like your life. Struggles, joys, victories, sorrows and defeats all live together in the same body and soul. But Jesus is Lord of all of these things.

There are times when a long and tiring day ends and I realize that tomorrow promises to be even worse. The only sustaining factor in my life or yours is that *God Is.* Outside of that reality, there is no hope.

While recovering from surgery recently, I became more depressed than I had been in months. I started to think of all the tasks that were unfinished and calling for my attention. This book was only about half written, and with school about to close, there were all kinds of things that had to be done. I had spent most of the day praying and crying. Finally, making an effort to overcome my paralysis, I got out some paper and started write letters.

As I started to write, I heard something fall to the floor in the kitchen and went to see what it was. I keep many of my favorite scripture verses stuck on my refrigerator door with little magnets so that I can memorize them and be constantly reminded of their significance. One of these had fallen, and when I picked it up, I saw that it was the verse from Isaiah about "renewing strength and mounting up with wings like eagles."

I made some smart remark about "being funny" to God. Somehow I got through the rest of the day. It wasn't easy but I made it.

The next day, Sunday, I still felt bad, but I managed to do a few things. Later that day I sat down at my desk to work and again heard something fall. When I went into the kitchen the same scripture was on the floor. I picked it up and said, "O.K. God, I get the point. I will try patience again."

"Coincidence" you say? You wonder why I am making such a big case out of this? Well, it is simple; I don't believe in coincidences, accidents or luck. I believe in a God who is involved in our lives and longs to speak to us and offer the riches of His love.

You may wonder why I have bothered to include a separate chapter on "waiting" in a book that also talks about suffering and patience. My point is that we can't ever learn the lessons of patience well enough to cease talking about them.

Society tells us we shouldn't have to wait. We push buttons and expect instant comfort or solutions to our problems. We move fast and we expect God to operate at our pace, but He doesn't.

The fact that God moves at His own speed causes us to be frustrated and even more impatient. He calls us "to wait upon Him" and "to hear His still small voice." I don't think "waiting" can be stressed enough as each of us seeks to respond to our call to be patient. Perhaps you have already learned some important lessons about waiting; if so, I am thankful for you. But I believe you will be asked to endure even more waiting as a result of your maturity. Regardless of where you are, don't forget that God is faithful.

Chapter 10

My Search for My Name

God took time during the summer of 1976 to help me begin the search for my name. My first school year at Mercer was completed and it should have been a happy time. I had a good job and I had accomplished some of my goals. I should have been content, but I wasn't.

I don't remember exactly how it all started, but I gradually began to deal with some issues in my heart and mind. It was agonizing. I was being forced to take a long hard look at some of my relationships with co-workers, my family and some of my friends. I realized that God was calling me to a different way of relating to people. He wanted me to live in a more open fellowship and to be more open with my life.

The problem was that I wasn't sure I wanted to be more open. It was hard to accept His new calling because I wasn't sure some of the people involved really cared about me.

The agony grew every day. It became harder and harder to keep going. There were days when my chest hurt from the emotional and spiritual pain in my soul. I didn't sleep very well. I had terrible nightmares. I was a mess.

I started to realize again, as I had before during my college years, that personal pain is no excuse for not being a servant. I had been called long before to servanthood, and the fact that there was still much yet to be healed in me did not mean I could refuse my calling. The pain was such that I wondered if anyone had ever died from the loneliness of this kind of struggle.

Many significant things happened in my life during this time and I want to try to share them with you. They are not easy to share because some of them are hard to remember. I think the memory problem reflects my desire to forget the pain.

My life to this point had been filled with activity. I was always reading, working, going places, talking to somebody or doing just anything to be busy. There were times when I was extremely active. I think I was this way because when I was still, I had to face some of my struggles. For a time I would face a struggle here or there, and then if I could, I would find some diversion from it.

There were times when my hyperactivity would make me so depressed I could hardly stand it. My emotional and spiritual life always had an up-and-down kind of motion. I was extremely sensitive and could be thrown into a depression that would last for days by a simple statement made thoughtlessly by someone.

I was afraid of being rejected or overlooked—far more than I needed to be. It was easy for me to believe that the people who cared about me were not really sincere.

There were many unhealed spots in my family relationships that hurt. I began again to deal with the relationship I had had with my daddy. There was much that had been left unsettled.

I thought about my mama and how we still had a lot to work out between us. I became afraid she would die before we could do it. I felt I was being challenged by God to become reconciled to my own family.

I believe reconciliation between family members is essential to the proper functioning of the kingdom, but it didn't seem possible it could happen in my family. There was still much distance between us in terms of both geography and emotion.

All of these thoughts and feelings crowded into my life for three months that summer. Somehow during this time, I started to feel a desire to slow down. Part of it may have come from being depressed, but I also think part of it was from God. I stopped running all over town. I stopped thinking of things I could do. My phone conversations began to diminish. I still watched television a lot, but that was about all I did.

I would go to work and come home. I often drove to Atlanta to attend church, but even that did not lessen the pain. However, there was a part of me that didn't want the pain to lessen. I felt there was some area of my life which needed to be healed and I did not want to get in the way.

I was very tired of running around in a frantic frenzy and being depressed all of the time. I thought surely there must be a place between those two extremes. I wanted to believe I could have more peace than I was experiencing, but that belief was hard to maintain for any length of time.

I stopped reading for awhile, a really significant act because it was not unusual for me to read three or four books every two weeks. I still spend every free moment I have reading, but then I was not motivated to read at all. I was tired all of the time and it was just easier to lie around and watch T.V.

Sometimes the T.V. programs were so boring that I paid little attention to them, but I needed the noise. One of the thoughts that haunted me was how alone I really was. Living alone does not have to be a bad experience, but it can be, and it was for me that summer.

Sometimes I would go out and forget for awhile how I felt. But as soon as I returned to my apartment, I would again feel the despair. It seemed always to greet me at the door. Some days were filled with tears. On other days the pain was so deep no tears could find their way through. I wondered, "What was to become of me?"

I knew that I not only had to get past this stage of my journey, but I also had to get through it on God's schedule. I was careful about what I did. There had been a time in my life when I had looked for quick answers. This time I didn't. I wasn't even sure there were any answers for me. Even if it meant staying depressed for the rest of my life, I didn't want any more of those "bandage-on-cancer" kinds of answers.

Those types of answers give a false sense of healing. All they have ever done for me is make me hyperactive, and after the hyperactivity, the depression is even worse.

People who care about you can do you a big favor sometimes if they let you suffer your pain and find help for it from God. Oftentimes we fail to allow people we love to experience the privilege of pain. Since more growth can take place in painful situations than at any other time, we should not try to insulate anybody from the opportunity for growth. But it is hard not to do because we want so much to serve.

There were some people who were willing to serve me by just being present whenever I needed them. But they never tried to take away my suffering.

Somewhere along the way I either came to believe that God would take care of me, or maybe I just hurt too much to care anymore. I still don't know which it was. I do know that I began to feel at times that if God had any power, He would do something for me. I didn't know what and I really didn't care. I waited.

He had been so faithful to me for thirty years that it was hard to believe I could be so filled with doubt and distrust. It proved, I guess, that we are never too old or too spiritually mature to doubt and to experience a crisis on our journey.

My prayers became very simple. I reached the point where I would get on my knees to pray and no words would come. There just was nothing else to say. He already knew all that was in my heart, but I didn't realize it at the time. I hurt too much to talk.

Late that summer I took a trip to Houston, Texas. I had certainly looked forward to getting away for awhile. I was going to attend a meeting, visit some members of my family, and see a friend from my college years. There was a little spark of hope in me that maybe something good would come out of the trip.

I think that hope began one afternoon when I was taking a nap and I didn't know if I were dreaming or not. Somehow I had heard Jesus say to me that there were many mansions for me in the house of the Father. The little dream ended quickly. When I awoke I felt peaceful—a feeling I had not had for more than two months.

The time for the trip finally came. I didn't take any books with me because I felt the Lord would decide how I should spend those seven days away. I stopped first in Atlanta to visit a friend, and while I was at her house, I glanced at Catherine Marshall's book, *Something More*. It began to speak to me, and I decided to take it along. That turned out to be a good decision.

Previous visits with my family had seldom been peaceful; there had always been a lot of struggles between us. I have always had trouble accepting them as they are, and that has never helped our relationship. I shared this struggle with my friend in Atlanta. She understood and promised to pray for me.

The day I left Atlanta was special. I was having a good day— the first in such a long time—and I was deeply grateful to God for it. It was a pretty day and there were a lot of clouds. I have always liked clouds, especially those fluffy white ones. They must be made from the dust the angels sweep from their houses. My flight from Atlanta to Houston went smoothly.

I dreaded arriving at a strange airport and taking a bus to the University of Houston campus where I was to attend my meeting. But it all went smoothly; God continued to reassure me that He was near.

The meeting was fine but not spectacular. I met a few people but didn't spend much time with them. The significant event of those days was my reading of *Something More*. It was used by God to show me that healing is really possible, and it helped me to end my struggle with the issue of tithing.

One of the things Catherine Marshall suggests is that you make a list of all the people in your life you haven't forgiven, then pray for them, and finally, work at forgiving them. I was surprised at how long my list was. I was surprised to discover I had such feelings of hostility toward several people. It was a very meaningful exercise. I also decided to tithe. Before I had always been afraid that I would decide to tithe and then not follow through. Somehow, as I knelt in that dormitory room at the University of Houston and made my commitment of giving a tithe to Him, I knew He would give me the courage to keep it.

After the conference ended on Thursday, I went to visit my brother and his family. It still was not easy to be around them, but I sensed myself accepting them as I never had before. Somehow they seemed different and I was not as threatened by them as I had been on some other visits.

My friend from college days came on Friday and I spent the night with her. She was having a few struggles of her own and she shared with me how she had prayed for somebody to talk to who might understand her problems. She said she had wished for a chance to see me. I was flattered that she had thought of me, and I was humbled by the fact that God had answered her prayer. Somehow, all other things that were happening that week were renewing my hope.

The next day, Adell—my sister who lives in Louisiana—came with her sons and daughter for a visit. We all seemed to enjoy just being together that evening. My niece was to celebrate her twenty-fifth birthday on Sunday. I woke up that morning and decided to bake a cake for her birthday. I Went out and bought all the ingredients. I was glad to be making a surprise for her. But I tried to take the cake from the pan too soon before it had cooled, and it fell apart. And so I had to go back out to a bakery and buy a cake. Sometimes it sure is hard to give!

When we gathered around my niece and sang happy birthday, the smile on her face made me grateful I had bought the cake. Then I almost cried when she said, "This is the first time I have ever had a cake for my birthday." The God who would go to the trouble of prompting an aunt to fix a cake and sing happy birthday to a twenty-five year old niece is a faithful God.

As I left Houston that Sunday afternoon, I was still at peace. When I found my seat on the plane, I wondered who would sit beside me. I used to worry about that because I always wanted to read on trips or just be by myself. But somehow on this Sunday I thought it would be all right to talk.

A nice man sat down beside me. He was on his way to Wichita for a meeting. I found out that he liked clouds too. We talked about them for half of the trip home. He also had a book of puzzles and we did some of those. I enjoyed very much spending an hour and a half with him that day.

The trip to Houston was significant in many ways. For one thing, my hope was renewed. I realized God hadn't forgotten me. I had often found myself being afraid He would not be faithful. It is a fear that still catches me by surprise sometimes. I hope I will be healed completely of it someday.

The end of August, I decided to go to Nashville and talk with my friend, Don Finto. I sensed a need to sort out some of my own problems. After a certain point, you need help from someone who can be more objective.

Don Finto is one of the most unusual men I have ever known. He knows who he is and that makes him free to help others affirm who they are. I needed to be affirmed and God used him in a special way to accomplish that.

We spent three hours together and his insights were tremendous. He made some suggestions about some things I needed to do. He helped me realize I had to accept everybody in my family just as they were. He helped me see I had not done that. I had been hoping they would change.

I still do hope and pray that several people in my family will change simply because they would be much happier. I no longer hope they will change just to make me feel better. That makes a difference.

About a month after seeing Don, I started to keep a journal. I began to record the thoughts, feelings and activities that were significant to me. Each night before going to bed, I would spend some time working on my journal, reading scripture, and sometimes praying. I slowly felt myself moving back toward a life having a little more fullness. I was very grateful.

I gained some insights as I walked through the valley that summer. Perhaps the most significant one was that God is faithful. Even when I don't know where He is or how He will take care of me, or even then I feel as if He doesn't remember me and doesn't really care, He is faithful!

I also realized that even though living can be a terribly lonely experience at times, being alone can still be a healing experience, too. I turned off that silly T.V. and started to seek silence. The oppressiveness of the previous silence was gone. For the time being at least, I had lost my fear of it. I started to enjoy my time of working on my journal and reading at nights.

I finally realized you can't have people near you all of the time. Even if you live with a whole group of folks, you need to have time alone. Remember how often Jesus got away from the crowd?

Sometimes we carry the crowd inside us, and the clamor does not allow us to hear the One who seeks us. Being alone has made me able to hear a few things I would not have heard a year ago.

I have seen some healing of my hyperactivity and depression. There are still times when I have to struggle to keep going. Those days will always come, but I don't have to be devastated by them anymore. I can go on even in those times. I know that because I am convinced nothing can ever separate me from God's love.

Recently, some students who came to my house to study said, "It is so peaceful here." No higher compliment could have been paid to a person like me who has spent so much time living like a hyperactive butterfly. For my house to be a place where somebody can experience peace is special fulfillment. And not only is there peace in the house, but there is peace in my soul as well. A dear friend once predicted that I would be a peaceful person someday. It must bless him to see the fulfillment of his prediction as he sees me a peaceful person.

It is amazing the things God can help you realize when you are being still and making some effort to hear His voice. I want to share one of these realizations with you.

A few months ago, some of us were discussing Idi Amin and the situation in Uganda. I very angrily said, "Somebody ought to kill that guy." It was a horrible thing to say, but a true expression of how I felt at the moment. A few days later while I was praying for Uganda, I started to think about Idi Amin and I could sense that God wanted me to pray for him. I said to God, "You must be kidding. Do You want me to pray that somebody will assassinate him?" I just couldn't believe God would want me to pray for a man like that. I supposed some pilgrim hundreds of years ago may have had the same reaction when God led him or her to pray for Saul of Tarsus.

At any rate, God made it clear to me that He loves Idi Amin. And then to make it worse, He said: "I love him as much as I love you." He loves Idi Amin because He made him and Jesus died for him. So while I must stand against the unrighteousness of Amin's atrocities, I can love him and pray for his salvation.

Another thing I was forced to consider was that if it were not for God's grace, I could be just like Amin. Given the same set of circumstances, I could be just like him. I am no better than the worst person alive without His grace. So who am I to criticize?

Spending time alone with God enables me to participate in community and fellowship, and during these times with Him, I learn that all of my sisters and brothers are just like me. I've learned I don't have to be afraid of them. I've learned I can know my brother and sister because I've finally realized I can know myself.

These times alone have also made me feel more connected to God who is the source of my strength. Being closer to God has made me more aware of myself and of those with whom I relate. This has been particularly true in my work as a counselor. I am now more aware of the person I am counseling with. I am more involved with him or her and have a deeper understanding of who she or he is.

God used the darkness and loneliness of the summer of 1976 to introduce me to myself in an even deeper way. There was nothing romantic about it, but it has become a creative force in my life. The power that kept me going was His grace and those gifts He had given me years before which had helped me hold onto life tenaciously.

As a result of those experiences that summer, I have come to know my name well enough to share my journey with you. If you have been blessed by my story, then you can join me in my thanksgiving to the Giver of all good and perfect gifts. God is to be praised because He gave me a promise and then led me faithfully through the wilderness to lay hold of it. Even though there were times when I felt He had withdrawn His presence from me, He was always there. He was there caring for me as He had been before in times of sorrow. I love God for the way He gives us what we need regardless of how we feel about it.

Chapter 11

He Knows My Name

I am finally able to realize the truth of this scripture: "For I am persuaded, that neither death, nor life, nor angels, nor principalities, nor powers, nor things present nor things to come, nor height, nor depth, nor any other creature, shall be able to separate us from the love of God, which is in Christ Jesus our Lord." (Rom 8:38, 39)

The journey I am on has been filled with many challenges and struggles, but it has led me to believe that "nothing can separate me from the love of God." The other thing my journey has made me realize is that God knows my name. God's involvement with my life, even before I knew that He existed, convinces me that He knows my name. If He knows you and me, then all is truly well.

As a member of an academic community, I hear the latest insights concerning the situation on our planet. Some of them are very frightening. We are ruining our world and we will reap death and destruction because of our disrespect for the environment and its resources.

As a community of believers, we have a responsibility to show more respect for our environment, our lives and our gifts. We need to fight evil wherever we find it. We need to take a stand against all that is unfair and unjust in the culture. But our standing as believers gives us a different perspective. Our hope is not in the economy or ecology. Our hope is in a living God and nothing can separate us from Him.

I refuse to participate in despair. It is a waste of time and energy. There are still those days when I am overwhelmed by the gravity of the world's problems, but I am called and committed to make a difference wherever I can. And so are you.

As believers who want to express the truth, we need to get involved with campaigns against torture; we need to be waging a war against poverty and hunger; we need to protest war itself; we need to fight against racism and sexism. Most of all we need to live personal lives of quality. Believing in Jesus Christ does not in any way exempt anyone from involvement in the struggles on this planet for dignity and the chance to live a decent life. But we go to battle because we are sent by Him and not because we have sent ourselves.

Recently, I was asked to call Bruce Edwards, the former pastor of the Plains Baptist Church, Plains, Georgia, to see if I could interview him. I called information and got his number, but as I wrote it down, I mistakenly changed one of the digits. I dialed the number expecting to reach the Edwards' home, but much to my surprise I got their neighbor and good friend, Pharis Walton, instead.

Pharis was a little hesitant to talk to me because there had been so many people calling. Ever since the 1976 presidential campaign, when a black man from a nearby town had gone to Plains and made an attempt to worship at the Plains Baptist Church, there had been tension. The man had been refused admission. The minister took a stand against this action and was fired as a result.

Pharis is a very close friend of Edwards and his family and had been experiencing sorrow with them. She and her family are members of the Plains Baptist Church.

All of the church's members who had wanted no blacks attending their church polarized themselves against those who thought the church should be open to any Christian. Much anger and hatred was being expressed among people who had professed to be sisters and brothers.

All of the anger and hatred had made Pharis feel rather bitter toward some of the people. She had decided to stay home from church for awhile. On the day that I "accidentally" got her on the phone by calling the "wrong" number, she had just been praying for some help. She told me, "I told God that I had to have some help; I just couldn't go on."

I called her that day because God was listening to her prayer and because He knows her name. He was able to use me to affirm her and to make her realize that there were black people who had been given new hope by her courage. We talked for about forty-five minutes. It was a beautiful time of fellowship on the telephone. Later I went to Plains and visited with her. She is my sister and I am grateful God gave us a chance to meet each other.

It is this kind of incident that makes it hard for me to believe in "accidents" in the lives of Christians.

A colleague of mine once asked me to deliver some Thanksgiving dinners for him because he had to be out of town. The dinners were to be delivered to some senior citizens. One of them went to Mrs. Lena Austin, a woman of ninety-one who lives alone and has no relatives.

I noticed, as I left her meal in the kitchen, that she appeared to have no other food in the house. I took the liberty of looking in the refrigerator and it was empty. I was appalled that this old woman sat alone in her two little rooms with no food and no hope for getting any.

Still, she seemed at peace. She was very friendly and talked about herself quite freely. I asked, "Why don't you have any food?" Her answer was simply that she had no money. Her welfare check just didn't cover everything. When her food ran out, she didn't have the money to buy more. I learned later that sometimes her next door neighbor brought her food.

A strong desire entered my soul to make life better for this woman. I wanted her to have a clean, well-lighted place with bright colors and nice smells. At times my value system can be as overwhelming as the problems of the poor, and I have to prayerfully remember that food is more essential than pretty walls or flowers. So, I went out and bought some food for her. She was grateful.

Now I am taking food to her on a regular basis, and I have become involved with her case worker at the welfare department because I think Mrs. Austin has been neglected. This case worker is probably overworked and tired, but I have difficulty being patient with her because of her attitude.

It makes me angry to observe Mrs. Austin's poverty and loneliness. But anger is not good enough; it's too much like crying. When you finish crying or being angry, you still must decide what you're going to do. I continually must remember that I have been called to action and not to paralysis caused by despair. And so I take her food and I pray for her. I share my life with her in all the ways I can.

Recently when I went to see her, I became particularly disturbed by how she is having to spend her last days on earth. She is almost blind and her arthritis is so bad she can hardly walk.

As I thought about her and her situation, a quiet thought began to develop in my heart about how God had been involved in making me a part of this woman's life. The fact that the God of the universe knows who she is and cares enough to send me to care for some of her needs is a beautiful testimony to His love. My presence in her life increases my faith that "nothing can separate us from the love of God."

One day Mrs. Austin told me, "It seems as if I have known you all of my life. You seem like you ought to be a member of my family." How precious for her to be so accepting of me. She has a beautiful spirit, and the gleam in her eyes and the quietness in her soul bless me.

Another example of God's faithfulness was shown me recently when my dentist discovered a cyst in my jawbone. This was upsetting since I had just completed more than five hundred dollars worth of dental work. The work had been done on the same side as the cyst and the dentist thought the two problems were related.

He sent me to an oral surgeon who told me I would have to enter the hospital to have the cyst removed. This made me even more upset. I didn't have time to be sick and I didn't want to spend money on hospital bills. The whole situation had me confused and I wondered how God would use this to glorify Himself. I decided He must have something special in mind.

There were a couple of days when I was sad about the impending surgery, but after those days passed I started to accept it. I began to consider the possibility of the doctor's finding cancer or something equally as serious, and I began to deal with the possibility of death. I finally concluded that nothing could separate me from God's love and I went to the hospital with confidence.

My friends all over the country had been praying for me, for the doctor, for the hospital personnel, and for all the people who would cross my path during the time of my surgery. I went into the hospital with a more peaceful spirit than I had ever had before in a similar situation. It was not resignation this time, but rather it was trust.

My hospital roommate was a very kind person. She, her husband and I had some nice conversations. And my doctor was a very sensitive man who believed in Jesus. He helped me overcome some of my distrust and fear of southern, white, male physicians. This surgeon accepted me and explained what he thought was going on inside my month. He was also willing to say honestly, "I won't know until I see the cyst and the biopsy report." I deeply appreciated his openness.

Everybody in the hospital was very kind to me. I developed a deep sense of love for all of the nursing staff and I was able to realize that God loved them and knew their names, too. On the morning of my surgery, I awoke early as usual. I spent the morning writing in my journal, praying, and reading some scripture. I felt that God was very near to me.

When they finally came and gave me the anesthetic shot, I was ready for surgery. It didn't take long before I began to feel drowsy. By the time I arrived at the operating room, I was nearly asleep. I made a few groggy comments in the operating room, but that's all I remembered until I woke up about two and a half hours later.

The surgery went well. My mouth hurt a little after surgery, but never enough to require pain medicine. My roommate in the hospital had her wisdom teeth taken out, and she had no pain or swelling either. The doctor said later, "What was in that room? I have never had people have as much surgery as you two without pain." I told him about all of the prayers for us. He was pleased.

Some friends of mine had wanted God to do the surgery *Himself* and save me from having to go through it. I told them I had no motivation to pray for that gift. I only wanted the gift that God had in mind for me. I've learned that if you try to dictate to God what you think your gifts should be, then you probably will be frustrated; but if you can accept whatever comes as a gift and be truly thankful to Him, then joy is easier to experience.

Many times we do have specific issues in our lives we want God to work out in specific ways. Those requests ought to be made, but we need to be careful and not forget to allow God the option of doing it His own way. By trying to dictate the kind of miracle that will be acceptable to us, we sometimes miss out on an even greater miracle.

I find this principle the hardest to accept during the times when I feel that if I don't get what I want, my life can't go on. It is always liberating to experience God helping me arrange those desires and setting me free to receive whatever He wants to give. It is liberating to realize that life goes on whether the miracles I am expecting occur or not.

There are thousands of examples of how God works in each of our lives. We just need to be looking for them.

My little friend Tami, for instance, had been praying for a puppy for a long time. She had asked her parents to get her a puppy, but they were waiting for the "right time"—you know, until after the yard was fenced and all the things were done that parents feel should be done before their children have pets.

One of the neighbors had a little puppy turn up at her house. The neighbor called the radio station and advertised the puppy, but nobody seemed to want him. Finally, he wandered down the street to Tami's house. Tami's mom told her to take the puppy home—and she did—but the neighbor invited Tami to keep the dog if she wanted him. So Tami came home with her very own little puppy under one arm and a box of "Puppy Love" dog food under the other. Her parents took one look at her face and knew they couldn't make her take it back. Later, when I went to see her puppy, Tami said, "See the puppy that God gave to me." It was a precious statement to come from the mouth of a ten-year-old child.

When I see the God of the universe involved this way in the life of a little girl, then I can believe that hope is realistic. Sometimes we have to take a long look at the simpler things in our world to really appreciate God. God's ways are not always as grandiose as our own tend to be.

The Lord Jesus is involved. He cares what happens to us. I have come to the conclusion that He knows my name. I am a very ordinary person. The fact that He knows my name does not make me unique. He knows your name, too. This story of my journey is your story as well. If you told it, you would have to change a few of the details, but the pain and the loneliness would be there.

The only way a person escapes pain in this world is by trying to avoid it, and in the long run, the avoidance of pain becomes more painful that the pain itself. *Suffering has been the most creative force in my life.*

As a black person, I used to think my ancestors had suffered so much that I shouldn't have to suffer. I thought I had suffered

enough during my childhood so that I shouldn't have to experience it in my adult life. How wrong I was. I know now that
suffering will last as long as I live, but so will joy.

God knows my name and your name too, and we have no reason to be afraid. Maybe the journey we all are on is not so much
for the purpose of God's finding us and learning our name, but
rather so that we can learn we have been found by Him and that
He knows our names.

Because we know God knows our names, we should be careful
in how we deal with people. They too are special in His sight. We
should ask Him to give us the grace to treat all people the way He
wants us to. It is not always easy, but if He is calling us to this
awareness, then He will give us what we need to answer the call.

The past year has been the best year of my life. I have sensed
God's involvement with me in ways that I have never experienced
before. Isaiah 60:1 has become very meaningful: "Arise, shine; for
thy light is come, and the glory of the Lord is risen upon thee."

I believe some new light has come to me and I am grateful. I
have felt a deeper sense of mission in my life and in my work than
ever before. I have become aware of some of my gifts, and I even
have been surprised that I have some of them!

I know that there will be more light in the future and that my
journey with Him will continue to be one of both joy and sorrow.
But I will go on in confidence that "nothing can separate me from
His love."

The other day, someone asked me about my future. I just
looked at them and admitted that I don't think about it much anymore. I am content with the realization that God knows my name.

God bless you, and have a good journey with Him.

Chapter 12

Having a Good Journey

Fifteen years ago I concluded the final chapter of my story with the admonition to my readers to "have a good journey." I hope and pray that those who may be reading this book again and those who are reading it for the first time are indeed having a good journey. May the reading of my book strengthen your life in whatever way that is good for you.

I am deeply grateful to God for this opportunity to share some of the threads that have been flowing together to weave my life for the past fifteen years since the first printing of *I Want Somebody To Know My Name*. It will not be easy to enclose the events of these past years in one chapter, but I hope to communicate the essence of them to you and to affirm the faithfulness of God to me as I have tried to faithfully participate in the weaving of my life tapestry thus far.

I first need to say that my mama died on May 8, 1993. My life has been deeply devastated by her death, and I am writing this chapter while I am in the midst of the greatest sorrow that my life has ever known. As you know, Mama and I had to work at our relationship, but, regardless of the hardships and struggles, over the years we had developed a deep connection to each other and much love and care. Mama was always on my side. She wished me a good life and worked as hard as she could to see that I had anything that would help my life to be good. She was very proud of me, even though she did not understand much of the work that I did. She faithfully attended all of my graduations, and when she saw my doctoral dissertation she said, "You sure did have to know a lot of words to write all of this." She was correct; I did have to know a lot of words. But all of those words seem so hollow when I attempt to use them to talk about Mama and her life, but I must try—both in this chapter and in a future book on African-American women and heroism.

For the purposes of this chapter, the most important point is that my life has been reshaped yet again—this time by the death of the most significant person to have ever been a part of my life. I am looking forward to the ways in which God will use this space of grief and sorrow to continue the work of making me into the person that He intended for me to be when I was given life.

Several other major events of these past years have impacted my life tremendously: my marriage to Modou Njie; the birth of my youngest son, William Sengarn; and the addition of my oldest son, Mbye Baboucar, to our family. In addition to the changes in my family structure were travels to the Middle East and West Africa, the completion of two degrees—a masters in clinical social work and the Ph. D., and a three-year struggle with rheumatoid arthritis.

Through all of these events, the clearest message that has emerged has been that God has called me to a journey that will always have tough choices and great challenges, but one in which I can trust that he will always be with me. I have been led to wonder at times if God remembers that I am here and if there will be "help coming in the morning." So far, whatever help that I have needed has been there.

After the publication of my story, I met many wonderful people, and many doors opened that I did not know existed. I was elated about all of the new opportunities. I was quite unprepared, however, for the heavy demand on me emotionally and physically. I came very close to losing control of my life because I did not know how to manage all of the newness—but God was faithful. This book had a purpose that was good and wholesome; it was not to be destructive.

In 1980 it became quite clear to me that I needed to become prepared educationally and to clarify my career goals. After much counseling, praying, and conversations with friends, I made the decision to return to school. I enrolled in an accelerated masters program in clinical social work at Atlanta University that I completed in eleven months. It was quite wonderful for me because I had prior experience in the mental health profession. The year that I enrolled in the accelerated program was its final year of existence, so it was clear to me that the grace of God had guided me onto a better path than I could have managed alone.

I graduated in 1981 and began to realize that I was feeling very unsettled and as if I needed to get away from North America. The feeling surprised me somewhat because I had not thought much about leaving the country. I simply told Jesus that I would do whatever was best for me, and that if I did not go anywhere I would try to understand what was creating my unrest and find other ways to handle it. In the fall of that year, an old friend from Chicago called and invited me to be a part of a Middle East study trip. I was speechless as I listened to him tell me that I just needed to get to New York and everything else would be paid. I had very little money so—had not the trip been paid in full—I would have had to decline it.

The trip to Jordan, Israel, and Lebanon was an amazing experience. My sense of the presence of Jesus as I walked around some of the places that He had been centuries before was astounding. I was struck dumb by the destruction of property and humanity in Lebanon. I will never forget the mass graves at Sabra and Shatilia, the site of massacres the summer before my visit; nor will I forget seeing in the hospitals the haunting faces of children with missing arms, legs, and eyes.

It was good to go away from home, but I must confess that I was very glad to get back to my little apartment on the campus at Mercer. The trip to the Middle East marked a new beginning for me in some very important ways. My heart was enlarged in terms of being able to care about others. Even though I cared about many others before it, I sensed that Jesus wanted me to see even more profoundly that there are so many children in God's family, and that it is very easy to ignore them, and that the ones in the Middle East needed not to be ignored.

I made speeches about the Middle East and participated in many consciousness raising activities after my return. I continued to read and try to gain a better understanding of what was going on there. That was very important to me. The restlessness I had before the Middle East trip did not leave me, however, and I began to realize that I wanted to travel some more, and that I needed to go to the land of my ancestors—West Africa.

I still had no money, but I felt compelled to look into the possibility of travel. I had decided that a year's rest after my master's work was completed was enough, so I applied to Emory University to begin work on my Ph.D. I was accepted and given a tuition grant to pay for the entire program. In the meantime, I inquired at Emory about Africa travel. I was told about Operation Crossroads Africa, a summer program that allows college students to work and travel in Africa. I was told that I could apply for the leaders program but that I would need to send to New York for further information and application forms.

After my conversations at Emory and as I was driving home from Atlanta, I prayed that God would help me to get to Africa or simply help me to find whatever else I needed to do if going there was not right for me. When I went into my office the next day, a packet of information from Operation Crossroads Africa had arrived in the mail. I held it in my hands, almost afraid to open it. I had never even heard of Crossroads until the previous day's conversation at Emory, and now I sat holding all of the information that I needed about that program.

Needless to say, I applied for the leaders program and was accepted to take twelve students to some African country. During orientation it was decided that I would go to Gambia, West Africa. I was told by the Crossroads staff that they talked of sending me to South Africa or East Africa but finally settled on Gambia.

Interestingly enough, that summer in Gambia I met Muhammad "Modou" Sengarn Njie, who was one of our Gambian counterparts. We fell in love and, after maintaining a year-long courtship that spanned our two continents, married eighteen months after we met in 1984. For the longest time, I had hoped to get married but was about to conclude that marriage was not in God's plan for my life, so I went about the business of my life as best I could and continued to try to be faithful. When I least expected it, my path crossed with Moudou's, and our lives were altered by the encounter.

It was hard being responsible for a group of college students in a developing country. Some of them were spoiled by the conveniences of home and not very flexible. Others in the group tried to roll with the punches. I often felt forsaken by God and everyone else as I tried to manage all that was before me. I cried a lot because it was very hard being in a strange land with all my responsibilities. When I am at the end of my resources, however,

I am then most able to see that Jesus is walking alongside me, holding me on the path to wherever I need to go.

Modou was indeed a gift not only to me personally but to our entire group. He helped us with language problems, currency exchanges (he worked in a bank), travel arrangements, and locating accommodations when we ventured away from our work site at Sapu. We travelled to Senegal after we completed our four-week work project in Gambia, and Modou's assistance was invaluable.

I spent the year after Crossroads fulfilling my residency course work requirements at Emory. The following summer, I returned to Gambia to visit Modou and his family and to do research on Gambian women and oppression. He came to the United States that fall, and we were married in November.

Even though I had managed to learn a great deal about community and sharing as a single person, I have been challenged through marriage beyond anything that I could have imagined. Needless to say, living with another person is rarely easy; anyone who has shared living space with another person knows that it can be very challenging. In the context of marriage, however, there is the relationship that comes from being together; the shared life has to encompass the individual and the collective journeys of the couple. In addition, we had the challenge of cross-cultural differences as well as a ten-year age difference. Two years after we were married, I gave birth to our son, William Sengarn. I was forty years old and completing my Ph.D. Modou was in college and not scheduled to graduate for another year.

When Modou graduated, several members of his family came from Gambia for graduation and brought his son Mbye Baboucar with them to begin his life in America with us. He was seven years old at that time. He has adjusted very well to being here and with us. He and his brother have become very devoted to one another.

Some of the time during the first years of being a wife and mother, I felt a deep disconnection from my former years of activism, spiritual disciplines, and the spiritual journey that I felt was mapped out for me. Perhaps the greatest lesson was yet to be taught to me, however—that God is not stagnant and that the Christian's journey cannot be stagnant, either. I believe that every aspect of my life has been verified by God's call, and that the true test of faithfulness is the continued willingness to follow—even when the set patterns that are comfortable and familiar are disrupted and challenged.

It was comfortable and familiar to be single. Responding to the challenge of marriage has disrupted that comfortableness. But is this not what we are promised by the Gospel? Our lives will not always be on smooth comfortable paths but, regardless of that fact, Jesus will be with us always.

Some days I long for the peace and quiet that I had before my family. I am challenged to find ways to reconstruct some of it so that I can write, pray, or simply be silent for awhile. But I would not trade the life that I have today with a partner who loves me and children who love me and the wonderful gift that it is for me to love them. They fill my life in a very special way. All that I really have to say about them is "thanks be to God."

The final challenge that I want to share with you is the physical challenge of rheumatoid arthritis. A stressful work situation seemed to be the initiating crisis for the onset of the arthritic process. I had misjudged a person in terms of ability to handle a working relationship. The process of realizing what a difficult situation I was involved with and managing to remove myself from it took about four months. It was like a long nightmare that I was not able to awake myself from. I want to hasten to say that my challenge is not to be overly focused upon the causes, but rather to concern myself with the lessons that are to be learned from yet another form of suffering and to look for ways to get well.

For the past two and one-half years, I have been determined not to become immobilized by arthritis. Many days have challenged that resolve as I have slowly made my way across the Mercer campus on legs that have not wanted to make the trip from my office to the classroom. On some days, my children have had to help me get my blouse on and off. I have been frightened by the pattern of this disease and the manner in which it seems to invade my life as if it has a mind of its own. In the past, I went to several doctors and discovered that the suggested therapies were made of harsh drugs with irreversible side effects. I tried some of them for awhile. Eventually, I decided that I did not want to try to cure one problem by creating many others. I felt a deep sense about trying to follow some type of alternative medical program. I exercise regularly and am on a weight loss program. I am not well, but I am eighty percent better than I was when I started on this program. My church has also prayed for me for over a year.

This illness has caused me to be depressed at times. It has been very expensive financially and emotionally. There are many lessons to glean from this space in my life, even though I sense that I do not comprehend what all of the lessons are at this time. I feel that the most profound truth is what I have known for a long time: Prayer changes things. The prayers have been not just for me to recover but that I might have whatever God intends for me. I think that God's intention has to do with healing in terms of my mind, body, and soul.

My exercise routine is something that I never was able to really commit to in the past. My attitude towards diet is very different; I have lost weight with less effort than I have ever exerted in the past. I have learned some great lessons about pacing myself so that I am forming a work and rest pattern that I have never had before.

In addition, I realize that the arthritis is teaching me more than I have ever known about being focused upon whatever I am engaging at the moment. I prided myself in the past with being able to attend to many things simultaneously, but this illness has taught me the value of being focused upon one activity or idea or thought at a time. The way in which the very quality of my daily life is enhanced by that focused attention is quite evident. I am sure that other lessons will become apparent as time goes on, but, for the moment, my attention is shifted from directly being concerned about the illness itself to other aspects of my life. As this is happening, the arthritis seems to be getting better.

As I conclude this effort at updating you on the years that have passed since 1978, I want to say very clearly that while much has changed for me, much has stayed the same. God's grace and involvement in steering the course of my life is certainly very much as it has been always. My sense of responsibility to God, myself, and others and my ability to articulate the ideas and particulars of the journey have gone through many transitions, however, and I have emerged a stronger and better person. My sense of inner clarity is far greater. I believe that my sense of myself as a person whose life is a gift both to myself and others is greater. I have less fear about being in this world as an African-American woman who has emerged from poverty and racism. I can trust that the ground upon which I stand is indeed intended for me.

My children have helped me to see more clearly than I did in the 1970s when I was first telling my story that only connection and faith to God and to one another will suffice in this life. I am at peace with myself today in a very quiet and special way. This does not mean that I do not have grave concerns about many issues. I still fight the battle with arthritis. I still grieve Mama's death. I will continue to have the trials of daily living. Confrontation with those hidden parts of myself that will be brought to the light will continue, and the revelation of them will cause me pain. But I will continue to trust that the gentle carpenter from Galilee will walk alongside me, and that no one will bring anything that he and I will be unable to handle. THANKS BE TO GOD!

Epilogue of Thanks

My appreciation goes to:

Jean Ruland

Thank you for your patience in typing those long over-crowded pages of yellow legal paper that made up the first draft of my book.

Linda Hilliard

God bless you for being willing to entertain out-of-town guests, take care of your family, and type the second and third drafts of my manuscript. It was evidence of your love for me because I couldn't pay you what it was worth to me to have you do it.

Carolyn Reynolds

Thanks for your patient editing of my manuscript.

Mercer University Student Personnel Staff

For not making me take a leave of absence while I wrote, thank you. Your support really helped.

The Community of Believers

To all of you who have loved me, prayed for me, and believed that God could use me to speak for Him in this book. Thank you! Some of you have cried with me and experienced the stress of this project. You were true friends through a time that was filled with both sweetness and frustration.

Peter Gillquist

My precious editor-friend who believed in me enough to insist that I continue to improve this book even when I was certain that I had no more to say. Thank you for your faith in me and your love for me.

Donald Wagner   You were the first person to suggest that I should write a book. You believed in me even on the days when I called you long distance and could only share doubts. You affirmed me by your patience and willingness to listen as I sorted out my feelings and memories. I appreciate you. Thank you.

Myra Davis Brown   Thank you for reading the first chapter of my first draft and encouraging me to continue.

Gordon Walker   Thank you for insisting that I write. Your faith in me has been important.

I love all of you and praise God for you.